Gravity Calling

By:
Jonathan

Gravity Calling
Book One of the Series *The Nine*
May 22, 2018, *First Edition*

Copyright © 2018

Cover Photo Credit: Filipe Almeida

All rights reserved. This book or any portion thereof may not be reproduced or used in any manner whatsoever without the express written permission of the publisher except for the use of brief quotations in a book review or scholarly journal.

ISBN-13: 978-1-942967-29-3

KreativeMinds Publishing
www.kreativeminds.net

Ordering Information:

Special discounts are available on quantity purchases by corporations, associations, educators, and others. For details, contact the publisher at the above listed address or the email address below.

U.S. trade bookstores and wholesalers: Please use the email address below. email: publishing@kreativeminds.net

To God, through whom all things are possible.

Always,
Jonathan

Introduction

...

While every word in this book is a true recounting of events that actually did occur, I cannot ask you to believe the words just because you have taken the time to read them. I can only ask that you approach the words with an open mind, no constraints, no preconceived boundaries, no judgment. If the words speak to you as much as the experiences have spoken to me, just listen. Somewhere in your inner dialogue, you will find a truth. If you find these words do not speak to you, that's okay too. As you will come to see, nothing can be impressed upon someone by force – only in the willingness to seek out and understand. Just know that these events were real and shared in verse as an effort to reveal hope to those searching for the greatness within themselves, and for those that have yet to begin their journey.

Always,
Jonathan

...

Prologue

Gravity.

Probably the most profound force we all long to feel. To be pulled in a direction; pulled toward a person; pulled to do the right thing; held in an orbit of certainty and peace. It is at the heart of trust, the heart of emotions – maybe even at the heart, just in general. We all search for it hoping to be pulled from the vacuum of life and into something greater than words can describe.

For most all of us, life will begin and end on this rock – ninety three million miles from our true life source; third in line to be fed the nutrients that allow us to thrive. It is miraculous to think that somehow, in the vastness of the universe, life came into being in this exact right spot. With every star, every planet, every moon – infinite options across the universe, life found a way to flourish. In this moment, we are not first in line and we are not last. We are right where we should be.

Regardless of a person's belief in the creation of our universe, our galaxy, Earth – the fact remains that against inexplicable odds, we are here. In this moment, just a speck of matter in the far reaches of the universe, we have meaning. We have purpose. We are alive. If we were not touched by the graces that once breathed life on Earth, we simply would not be.

Much in the same way the Earth has formed and has flourished, every person's walk in life is a special convergence of great odds. Career success, Love, loss, family, friends and wealth all tend to define a person's happiness and inner peace. We are all on a quest for reason and understanding. We all hope to find our significance that brings our souls to an inner harmony – more specifically, the feeling when we know our life is in balance with everything around us. But, the reality is only a few people find it. The vast majority of us will likely never allow ourselves to find true harmony. On the surface, it may sound a little distressing and pessimistic. And in many aspects, it is not the Cinderella story that so many children are raised to expect. But that is what makes the Not-So-Cinderella journey beautiful. For in our quest to find happily ever after, we often lose track of the journey – and the journey is what makes the ending worthwhile.

So, this is where the story begins – a story not about finishing first, not about finishing last, but about being caught somewhere in between – searching for any sense of gravity to pull us into where we are meant to be.

Genesis

Darkness. That was the first thing I saw when I opened my eyes. The sky, the Earth, and everything around me was blanketed in a black pitch that shielded my eyes from seeing – but most importantly, from feeling – any sense of hope. This was the first time I felt truly lost; no sense of wonder, no sense of direction. The density of the blackness was suffocating. With each breath I took, I felt the space close in around me – even more than I thought was ever possible from the previous exhalation. With every breath in and every exhalation, the blackness grew darker than before – denser, thicker, heavier – impossibly so; becoming increasingly more difficult to render the next breath.

My mind raced at the possibilities. As a child, we often lay upon the ground on cloudless nights staring into the far reaches of space – the darkness of the skies. To see the stars twinkle in the atmosphere causes the mind to erupt into endless wonders of potential. Through the darkness, light has travelled unfathomable distances just to let us know that we are not alone. We are amongst a great ocean of stars, just like our own – in the magnitude of billions upon billions. Through a child's eyes, we can sense just how small we are yet still manage to find a familiar comfort in the twinkling lightshow above us.

Gravity Calling

Through a child's eyes – even without intention – we allow each lightdrop to be a measure of hope – a beacon that speaks to our innermost voice and encompasses our minds in wonder, hope and dreams. But this darkness was different. There were no beacons calling out from the blackness. There was nothing to cling to for security or strength.

In this darkness I knew not what to search for, only that I should be searching. Desperately at times and on the verge of giving up many times over – all I longed to see was a pinhole of light; a glimmer, a glint – something that I could mentally hold onto to lead me home. Why and how I found myself in the darkness could be explored later. The only thing that mattered was survival and finding familiarity with something, anything that could be used as a compass on my journey, so that one day I could find my way out.

...
For me, this is how it started.
This is how it all began.
This was my Genesis.
...

This darkness was my second birth; the beginning of creation of what I am today; a start that had to be founded upon a life that pre-existed – and one that will undoubtedly go on to stretch beyond the bounds of the duration of my physical experience. Though I would not recognize it as such at the time, all I would come to know from those moments was a sense of

Genesis

searching, a sense of direction, a sense of primal survival that had been awakened deep within the inner reaches of my very being. On the outside, people would not see the same man I saw standing amidst the crumbled pieces of a life that once was. They would only see strength and hope. On the inside, though, there was only blackness; thoughts nonchalantly tossed around seeking reason; a mental flailing of anything and everything in an effort to gather my bearings. This is not how I would have ever expected a Cinderella story to begin – and perhaps that is why I think the journey is more appropriately called a Not-So-Cinderella story. For in all great things, the journey must first unveil what once was in order for a person to understand what will one day become – and in that, hopefully grant the serenity, peace and overflowing abundance of Love that we all hope to one day experience in our lives.

First Birth

To understand where the Not-So-Cinderella story begins, one must first understand a portion of the history leading up to this place in time. For me, this place in time begins with an otherwise cataclysmic ending to a life that once was. It was a life built around a marriage that I was naively blind to the ending's approach, and painfully optimistic in hope that better days were just a sunrise away. I say painfully optimistic because I am sure that if anyone was able to observe my life from the inside as I saw it, they would have undoubtedly seen the ending looming ahead. It was as if I was driving ninety miles per hour into a hairpin turn I never saw coming. I missed the signs. I missed the warnings. I missed the flashing lights. I was so much on cloud nine that I could not see three feet in front of me...and there was no chance for recovery.

My life began right on time. I was born on the day and the hour the doctors initially projected. Throughout my life, every challenge, every goal, every award, every life milestone – really anything I ever set my mind to, or was ever told I needed to accomplish – I did...just like clockwork. I had my first job at fifteen. At sixteen I was paying for my gas and expenses. At seventeen, I graduated high school near the top of my class – a year earlier than most. Due to a battle with mono my freshman year in college, I missed one semester and ended up transferring institutions, yet still managed to graduate in four years – which was actually three and a half years of classes. I did all of this while working forty hours a week, maintaining my GPA for scholarships, taking overloads each semester in order to play catch-up and, oddly enough, never buying or borrowing a single book for any of my classes.

Having just actually put those years of my life into words, I can only look back and grin, because it definitely defied the odds of most high school and college experiences. However, I can never view any of those days as anything other than what was supposed to happen – only what I expected of myself. I accepted those years as "what people do." Never did I complain, nor did I have any reason to think my life was coasting along in any other way than it was supposed to. It was just what I had come to understand about the mechanics of my life. Even when I set unbelievably high goals for myself, I always managed to achieve them.

It would only seem natural to have met my now ex-wife, Stacey, during my senior year of college. After all, my parents married immediately after college when they were twenty-two & twenty-three. As many children are raised, I too was brought up believing in a situational timeline for graduating college, marrying, beginning a career, buying a house, having children, saving, retiring, etc...the list goes on and on. It was not as if I molded my life to the timeline, but rather the events of my life unfolded according to the timeline. I always figured

First Birth

I must be doing something right because every single piece had fallen into place...just like clockwork.

The day I met Stacey, I knew there was something special about her. I could go in so far as to say that the fraction of a second that my eyes met hers, just before she glanced down and away to pretend as if she had not looked my way, was the moment I knew she was the one. I was twenty years old and managing one of the largest music venues in a bustling college city – and this is where our eyes would first meet.

Little Red Star

At twenty years old, to assume my social life took a backseat to the forty-hour workweek would be a misnomer. In fact, my job blurred the lines between business and my social life due to the thousands of college students I saw and interacted with on a nightly basis. But therein created a major dilemma for me. While I enjoyed everything about my job, somewhere in my mind I had created a set of guidelines for when, where, and how I would meet the girl I would one day marry. I lived by my rules. They kept my life in check. So for me to date anyone from places or situations outside of the scenarios I had envisioned was not even a question – it was a hard line drawn in the sand. As irony would have it, I was standing in the back of the venue managing a crowded Thursday night when I first saw the woman I would one day marry.

To understand how conflicted I was at that moment would be hard for anyone to fully comprehend without a brief background on how I believed I would one day meet the girl of my dreams. Keep in mind that everything I had ever set my mind to accomplish, happened just in the manner in which I planned. Even if slightly a dreamer at times, I set unbelievably high goals, and with the right effort, expected to achieve them. In the end, I often did achieve the unachievable, and if I fell short, I would pick myself up and keep trying until I reached the goal. Failure had never been an option...and I almost always took this for granted. And never did I bend the rules to achieve my desired results.

So when it would come to finding my happily-ever-after, it was only appropriate that all I had ever known were two parents that had been married for twenty-two years, two sets of grandparents that had managed to remain happily married for close to fifty years a piece, as well as the greater influence of being raised within a Christian-inspired and Disney-influenced household. With having my life seemingly unfold to a situational timeline like clockwork, I could only expect that finding my happily-ever-after would happen in the manner I was raised to expect. Why would I even question a situation to the contrary?

Take any Dianne Warren song, any epic Love story, any movie, any fairytale, or any combination of the above and apply that to a person's life. Is it possible? Could someone's life actually be that remarkably similar to the euphoric fiction we witness in our pop culture? In retrospect, probably not in the sense I just described. And as I would eventually come to find out, it happens in a way that euphoric fiction can't even approach – but that is another story. At this particular time though, I was blindly optimistic that my life would play out to a chorus of "I can show you the world, shining, shimmering, splendid..." The Disney fairytale was far from just a reality – it was an expectation. And in those fairytales, social settings were never where true Love was found.

Little Red Star

I viewed the search for my soul-mate as an epic journey into the unknown. I knew without a shadow of a doubt that there would be a moment of absolution in the first few seconds of crossing paths with this girl. I wasn't just a stereotypical believer in Love-at-first-site. My soul's very foundation was based on the concept that every other girl I met had little to no chance of having any significance in my life beyond just a friendship. I rarely dated just to date. And from the outside, I was the only guy I knew saving himself for marriage.

I imagined every woman's name on a list...all three and a half billion of them. Young or old, race or ethnicity, impoverished or wealthy, it did not matter. If you were a female, your name was on this list. I believed that somewhere on this list of three and a half billion names printed in black ink, there was at least one that had a red asterisk beside it. This little red star represented everything for which I was searching. I would have no questions about this girl – I would know that she was the one intended for me, and I for her.

Unlike others I knew who would date the first person that showed them potential, explore the situation for a few months, then move on to the next person, I figured I needed to make pace through the metaphorical list of names. After all, I had lived my life overly efficiently – a clockwork-like goal achiever in every sense of the definition. Three and a half billion names could take some time to sort through. I never discussed my "list" with anyone, and I am ultimately glad I never did. It was probably just assumed that I was on the quest for the impossible and that one day I would wake up and realize I had wasted my time and should have settled on someone with whom I could have been compatible. But to me, my list was a visualization of the concept of God's divine architecture – the grand design of how spiritual bodies fall into harmony with one another.

In my haste to make headway on my list until that moment I would cross paths with that little red star, I rarely made it past "hello" with another, or perhaps even a general acknowledgement of their existence. I didn't do so rudely. In fact – it was quite the opposite. I managed to make friends with nearly everyone I met – but I kept to my own. I could sit in a class in college with twenty girls and by the end of class be spiritually aware that these twenty girls did not represent the red star on my list. I assume if someone was aware of my thought process at that time, I would likely have been viewed unfavorably. But that is the funny thing about spiritual recognition in another. Words are not required. Only within the spiritual recognition in another do words become important. I allowed my spirit to become the driver and my mind and body to listen for its conversation with another.

To another, the eyes are the deliverer of their reality. The image of the person who falls into view; the sound of that person's voice fills their ears in attention; the touch that ignites the skin when bodies make contact. And while each of those senses holds a rightful place in our earthly walk to amplify the sensations of the world around us, the spiritual recognition in another is an awareness of a specific feeling deep within the soul that ignites the outermost boundaries of the heavens when two souls collide. Though I had not experienced it ever before, I somehow already knew how the feeling would course through every part of my body.

But for everything I thought I knew – the first time I would cross paths with the girl whose name had that little red star next to it, would cause every thread of stitching to my soul to come undone. In that moment, all I would come to know is that every bit of waiting until that day, every bit of anticipation leading up unto that point, could not have prepared me for the undeniable realization of truth that unfolded before my eyes. The only way I can help illustrate that moment is to compare it to one of the most critically acclaimed movies of all time – Schindler's List. Imagine a black and white scene where a little girl is walking through a crowd in a red coat. The red coat is vibrant, and one of the only splashes of color in the movie during the entire three hours. Every bit of attention is drawn to this girl as everyone and everything else becomes insignificant in the background. Movie context aside, that moment where all focus was placed on that girl and everyone and everything else lost significance is how I felt the very moment I realized I was staring at that red splash of color on my list. Without a spoken word, I knew before we even said hello.

Rules Are Meant To Be Broken

Over the coming months, an internal struggle ensued where I began rationalizing the very rules I had in place for my life. Nothing could have prepared me for this internal conflict over those months. As I began to see Stacey out and get to know her more, I realized the rule I had put in place as to where I would meet my soul's counterpoint would eventually have to crumble out of its very own existence. I could not fight fate – and it became more obvious with each passing moment. She would go on to become the one exception to my rule and the only exception that would ever be needed.

I began to learn that preconceived notions on artificial boundaries are just that – notions. They are ego's attempts to place controls on the uncontrollable. Up until that point in my life, everything I had worked so hard to accomplish had been accomplished with some form of mental boundaries. It seemed necessary for me to adhere to these "rules" in order to accomplish the next steps required on my journey. For some reason, I had falsely assumed that the same artificial rules and boundaries I had placed on my journey would be mirrored in whomever my soul found harmony. But nothing could have been further from the truth.

    The reality is that ego-driven earthly goals require self-imposed rules; rules that require boundaries in order to accomplish earthly wonders. But the spirit is not bound by convention, thought, or constructs of the human mind. The spirit is only bound by the divine architecture of God's creation. And, within that divine architecture is the potential for anything and everything possible. To this point, I still had the misguidance that I was in control of my spirit and that it could be bound by the artificial boundaries I chose to place in governance over it. It would take over a decade of growth before I would begin to understand the error of my ways. But, that is not important yet. For this point in my journey it is only necessary to understand that I had blind faith that I was acting in what I perceived to be the will of the Almighty.

    As the days mounted from the moment my eyes first saw hers, so did the very pressure for me to allow the boundaries of my thoughts to fall from their existence. I realized that rules were never meant to bind the soul – only to serve as guidelines until the truly extraordinary comes along. If there are rules in place for the soul, those rules are meant to be broken. For to be bound by rules is to second guess the extraordinary hand and overpowering presence of a divine moment. Every day Stacey grew more beautiful – a feat that seemed impossible from the amount of beauty I saw in her from the very first moment. Our conversations drew on my soul, pulling it in closer to hers. If there is a fabric of existence, I can only imag-

Rules Are Meant To Be Broken

ine a divine hand at work, taking needle and thread – binding our souls together. When I learned that her birthday was drawing near, I decided that was the opportunity I needed – the doorway to exit the rules I had in place and explore the divine unknown. I used that opportunity to ask her out for the first time. And, for the first time, I was now sailing into the uncharted waters, guided only by the North Star to my soul.

The Fast, The Rare

From the outside looking in, I am sure every friend and family member must have been caught off-guard. After all, for the past twenty years I had only dated a couple of girls with no relationship lasting longer than a few months. Truthfully, when dating at a younger age, the time spent together may have only been equivalent to a few days or weeks together. As people grow older, time spent together is easier to manage. In youth, we are bound by parental schedules, school, driver's licenses, curfews, and part-time minimum-wage incomes. So from an outside perspective, my life changed directions very quickly. To me, it was the absolute ride I wanted to be a part of – a roller coaster that I boarded into the unknown, traveling at breakneck speeds into uncharted emotions.

The day I took Stacey out for the first time, was the first moment I realized I was not in control of my life. I no longer had control of the emotions, the thoughts, the desires. The situational timeline my life had found itself adhered to had now taken a mind of its own. I could not stop its impeding stronghold on my life. In the scheme of things, I am sure it appeared as if this was just another circumstance that defied all odds and just "worked out" in my life. Every friend who thought I was on a quest for the impossible girl was now laying witness to just another seemingly fate-driven moment for me. After all, everything was happening like clockwork, as it always had. It was the end of my senior year of college and I had met the girl I was going to marry.

From the first night we went out, we rarely spent a moment apart. Even separated by an hour's distance in drive time, we managed to see each other at every opportunity. Though her mother and father chose not to ask too many questions, she rarely spent any days at home. We met in December, went out in March and by June we were virtually living together. In May I graduated from the University of Georgia with my bachelors degree and was already talking to my father about engagement rings and how to approach the next steps in my life with her. I could go as far as to say that I knew the moment our eyes met that she was the one. I could have married her that day, but it would have defied all earthly practicality about first experiencing the companionship of another. This was no ordinary moment – this was the fast, the rare.

Days together turned into weeks. The weeks turned into months. By August I moved into her home town and took a job that paid enough to get by. It covered our expenses and allowed her to concentrate on school without worrying about having to work. By November we were engaged – merely eight months after we first went out. Though our finances were very tight, we managed to pay for our wedding in May without having to rely on family members. It wasn't that family members didn't offer to help. It was just that we didn't want to pass

The Fast, The Rare

the burden of cost onto others if we had the ability to cover the costs. We did receive our honeymoon trip as a gift and her family helped with the wedding dress and accents. Most thankfully, her family spent a tremendous amount of their available time helping make decorations by hand to help save on costs.

We put together a gorgeous wedding. We were married in a large rustic building with beautiful, exposed rafters. Candlelight lit the reception tables and homemade bouquets donned the aisles for the bride to walk down. Family came from all over the surrounding area to attend the ceremony. For us to have lived in such a remote part of Georgia, I was overcome with amazement to see my entire family and relatives help fill the building. Her family and relatives were all local, so there was no challenge filling the building to its capacity. All in all, the number of guests totaled a little shy of a hundred – nearly as many as we invited. I could never have asked for a more beautiful way to say "I do" to the woman I planned on spending the rest of my life with. We could have spent a hundred times the meager amount we spent on the wedding and would not have created any better atmosphere than the one that was present that day.

As would seem to be the theme of everything "just working out" in my life to this point – even the spectacularly romantic setting, perfect flowers, music, food, gifts, table centerpieces, dress, building reservations – the entire wedding only totaled in expenses under a third of the most inexpensive/budget weddings I have known. Mostly, this can be attributed to the hard work her family put in with handmade decorations and the hand-stitching of her dress. And, perhaps it was in how every aspect of the wedding had so much Love and care poured into every detail – all the way down to the hand-stitching – that caused the entire wedding to be filled with such beauty – a radiance that cannot be fully quantified to the eye, but only to the soul. Everything managed to fall into place. It was apparent to everyone that our Creator was filling our lives, our very surroundings with His warmth and grace, blessing us with each step we took forward into His presence. We drove off into the sunset with a lifetime of memories already made, new memories left untold, and experiences to fill our hearts with awe and wonder.

Counterweight To Love

At first blush, everything leading up to that point in my life seemed Cinderella-esque – and that is the stage I had to set for you as the reader. But, as the old adage goes: nothing is ever quite like it seems. On the surface, I had experienced a lifetime of everything "just working out." It was due to this anomalic journey, that I had no other reason to expect anything would, much less should, happen any other way than our pop culture would lead us to believe.

The next five years of my life I would eventually come to define as a journey in becoming a personal counterweight to Love. That is not to say that I did not experience Love. By every written and unwritten definition, my body and soul became so enraptured in the very essence that it was often overwhelming to function in the real world. Reality became so distant that even a mental break from my emotions seemed like a mundane visit to a third world country. But Love is just that – an overwhelming feeling and connection in another. The fairytales and movies on which we are raised, fall short in explaining the ensuing journey that inevitably takes place once the soul finds its counterpoint in another. The next five years of my life would become a rough lesson in understanding this journey.

Gravity Calling

By definition, Love is:

"1) a strong affection for another rising out of kinship or personal ties; 2) warm attachment, enthusiasm or devotion; 3) the object of attachment, enthusiasm or devotion"

- Merriam-Webster's Dictionary

To fully understand the dictionary definition of the word "Love" one must put aside all preconceived notions of how we as humans explain Love. For a person who so blindly believed in the fairytale Love story, I fell victim to not properly understanding this paradox. I would have described Love as the very actions associated with loving someone – and indeed, most people would as well. For instance, and probably a very typical explanation of Love is when a person will sacrifice everything for the other, including his or her own life. But, as my journey through the next five years of my life helped me understand, Love is not defined by our actions. To me, the actions are better defined as a counterweight to Love – the actions we take in order to preserve and safeguard the ones we Love. The relevance of this distinction is important to understand, because just as a scale has a counterweight, Love, too, must too have a counterweight to balance its gravity. Any tilt in this scale will undoubtedly create a chasm that is difficult, if not impossible, to bridge.

Counterweight To Love

The truth is, no soul is ever given to another – even in Love, for no soul can ever be had. Souls can only find harmony with another and maintain that beauty and brilliance for as long as each person moves forward on their personal journey while ensuring their actions match Love's counterweight needs. Love is a song in motion wherein all of the notes continue to fall into place in time and melody – sometimes by design, sometimes by chance, but always in beauty and mystique. The moment a person first falls in Love is the moment that the journey in becoming a personal counterweight to Love begins. For me, that moment was not the moment when everyone and everything else faded away and Stacey first fell into the spotlight of my eye. That particular moment could be better described as the moment I gave myself a chance to Love. And while pop culture leads us to believe that Love at first sight is true Love, I had always been of the opinion (at that point) that a person could not truly see a person from a distance, only sense presence and potential of their heart and soul. To see a person's heart is something I needed to experience – and it was only then that I believed I would truly know that I fully Loved somebody the first time. Through faith we find reason. And, though I knew Stacey was the one for me at that point on the journey in my life, I had to understand reason to rationalize the faith I already knew – an important distinction for that point on my journey.

For me, the second time Stacey and I went out was the moment that will forever be etched into my memory as the moment I knew I was in Love. As a person who believed in the fairytale, I never questioned why I did not allow myself to fully fall in Love on the first date. In fact, I was entirely confident I was falling in Love the moment I first saw her. But, if falling in Love is the leap, knowing you have completely fallen in Love is pulling the parachute – and everything else after that moment is just the glide home that takes your breath away.

 As vividly as the day it occurred, I can still replay each minute leading up to that moment I allowed myself to Love. It all began with Stacey driving to meet me at my apartment for our second date. It was the second time she had visited my apartment, but the first time she had driven from her house. I would come to learn that directions were not one of her strong suits – and it was actually one of those little things I came to adore about her. I could also tell she was entirely self-conscious about having to call and ask me for directions, which made me smile a little on the inside. Her first phone call on her way to my apartment was innocent enough – just making sure she understood the directions to my place. By her second call, I could tell she was entirely lost and trying to downplay how unaware of her surroundings she was. Her third call was almost panicked – but in an undeniably cute way to me. When she realized she was in the wrong place and needed to turn around, she pulled into a Captain D's parking lot. In the midst of our conversation a sudden, crashing sound could be heard followed by complete silence. My heart stopped as all I could only envision was the worst. After several agonizing seconds, I could hear her shaky voice confessing she had just driven over a parking curb. While she never admitted

Counterweight To Love

it, I can only envision the tears welling up in her eyes, her face flushed and the hollow embarrassment she must have felt in those moments on the phone. If the tables were turned, I know I would be entirely embarrassed of myself. But, she never managed to lose her composure. Once she became comfortable with the remainder of the directions, we ended our phone call – only a few minutes before my doorbell would eventually ring.

    The events of that day all became a blur of emotions after I opened the door. This was the moment – the moment forever etched into my memory. It is funny how in just a fraction of a second, time stood still and I was able to capture every little detail, every nuance of that moment into the deepest recesses of my memory. It was as if I was staring at a picture and some greater power decided to allow me all of the time in the world to just stare – to soak in everything, every intricacy, every bit of intimacy, every shadow, every sound, every scent. It is the only memory created unto that point where I could say with complete confidence that I could recall every single sense I experienced in the moment.

    As I opened the door for her, the fraction of a second she glanced up from the ground and her eyes caught mine was the moment that took my breath away. Every bit of composure she maintained on the phone was totally lost in her eyes as they met mine. One look, one glance, a flash of her eyes that lasted only a fraction of a second, was all it took to open the floodgates to my soul. It was in that moment I could see everything she was thinking, everything she was feeling, everything

Gravity Calling

that she was trying so hard to mask and not let me see. In that split second, I was able to see and experience her heart and soul down to its very core. It was one of the only moments of certainty in my life, and the first moment of certainty I had ever experienced.

This was the moment that would set into motion the next seven years of my life: the decisions, the financial ups & downs, the career choices – every major decision in my life would be centered around this tiny grain of time; insignificant in every aspect to everyone else. For me, this was the moment. For everyone else, it was just another passing nod to the Earth's rotation around the sun, a moment only giving way to a forgettable next. But that is how time works – it's only relative to the observer, and measured in brilliance unto the unseen. For me, this was the moment that the path for my journey as becoming a counterweight to Love began. Though I did not recognize it at the time, my life would forever be shaped by the way our souls collided and the way we would each handle our particular roles in the grand design to being a counterweight to Love.

Hairpin Turn & Flashing Lights

The ensuing months from when we said, "I do" became a whirlwind of puppy Love and newlywed afterglow. Though I tried to downplay to myself the epic romantic saga that I was experiencing within – all I could ever visualize was my body serving as the walls to an uncontrollable sense of great energy tidally locked to her spirit. It was as if my body contained a great ocean within its walls that was pushed and pulled with the motion of our souls experiencing each other's orbit. It was a force greater than I had ever known – one that I wasn't quite ever sure how to experience in small doses. Everything was such a rush that I longed with each moment to experience it more. Like a drug or an addiction to adrenaline, I always wanted more. I needed more. There was no rationality in my mind to experiencing this feeling in any other way than soul naked, fully opened up, pedal pressed to the floorboard, speeding off into the burning sunset.

Perhaps the greatest lesson during our time together is that the desire to feel more, blurred my vision along this portion of my journey. For, the faster a person moves in relativity

Gravity Calling

to his surroundings, the more blurred the surroundings become. It becomes easy to miss the signs along the highway, the flashing lights warning you of your speed leading into the hairpin turn – blind to the details, oblivious to the likely crash ahead. To the driver, the blurred signs and streaks of lights whizzing by in the periphery are like shooting stars and Northern Lights – their very meaning obscured behind the wishes, hopes, and dreams in the magic that their beauty entails. Though I have to believe that the experience of Love in that way has to exist somewhere in the universe when two like souls collide – the kind of Love that will only continue to grow and amplify in light when both people are not afraid to Love uncontrollably – during this time I gave no caution to the signs and the flashing lights and flew into the hairpin turn oblivious to its existence.

From the outside, Stacey and I had quite possibly the most perfect of marriages. To others, we were a young Love that would stand the test of time. The future held within it imagery of that ninety year old couple that still holds each other's hands and romantically feeds each other food from time to time. It was every Nicholas Sparks novel ever penned, but without the tragedies – a hopelessly, helplessly, fairytale romance. But, obscured from the vision of those that saw us together, was a young Love experiencing everything a young Love could possibly experience: the good, the great, the happy, the sad, the unknown – but most importantly, the lessons in becoming a counterweight to Love.

Hairpin Turn & Flashing Lights

The actions of a counterweight are often discreetly hidden from the eyes of others. A counterweight is a small object with great mass used to counter the pull of gravity and ease the burden of the one bearing the counterweight and the gravity combined. Counterweights are used on sliding scales, on shoulder mounted video cameras and lighting equipment, on cranes and other construction equipment that move great objects. They are found on nearly everything that carries any significant payload on Earth. The counterweight is necessary to allow these types of machines to function, so they do not topple over in effect from the forces acting upon them.

Like unto a counterweight, the actions we take in our daily lives affect every aspect of our surroundings. Each motion, movement, look, gesture – all affect, for better or worse, those standing in our presence. And for those standing and observing from afar, the ripples from each action still eventually manage to reach the observer's shoreline. Within every relationship, our proximity to one another is much closer and therefore our actions are much stronger in effect to the other. Every action holds that much more significance in intent, purpose and impact to the ones we care about the most. And the greater the extremes, the greater the amount of work that will be required as a counterweight to keep Love's harmony in balance. But counterweights should not be mistaken for magnetism. For just as a magnet requires a north and south pole to attract, like poles cause magnets to repel. Our words and actions are like magnets unto the soul. Just because two souls find harmony together, does not mean that the words and actions do not hold the potential to drive the two apart. On the contrary, two souls can be in perfect harmony while the words and actions serve to either strengthen or weaken the song the souls create together.

During our marriage, every action I took was filled with the utmost care and respect for the ripples it could create. I'm sure at times I faltered along the way – everyone does – but I always took the time and care to ensure I was moving forward in our relationship. I never felt a need to argue, so fighting words were never introduced or entertained by me. If there ever was conflict, I wanted to talk through whatever the situation would be in an attempt to find the best resolution to the problem. I never yelled. I never exerted anger, for I could not understand how anyone could ever be angry at the one they Loved. I could experience disappointment and strife, but never anger. It just never registered in my book. And, I always lived by the rule to never go to bed with anything left that could fester in the mind. Just as sores can fester on the body, sour thoughts will fester in the mind when left unaddressed. I believed in "I Love you's" and "I'm sorry's" and holding each other as you fall asleep. But this is where we differed – and not that one of us was right, or one of us was wrong. We just were not in sync on those thoughts. In those same scenarios she believed in avoidance, not talking, and cold shoulders at the end of tough conversations. And somewhere within conversations, the fuel for anger could quickly be fed. To this day I could not tell you a single reason she went to sleep mad, which should indicate that the issue was never in the object of the anger, but within something personal, or within the fading Love itself.

    Throughout the years, I came to learn that conflict resolution only works when both parties strive for the same goal. The counterweight involved has to be balanced from both sides. And unfortunately, hers and my intents were never quite aligned. This doesn't mean that one party had to be right or wrong, but rather that the common goal should have been to find peace and harmony within the situation, and quite often that was not the case. Too often couples believe that one of them must be correct and the other wrong, thus giving rise to angst and dissonance between the two. The trick is to work with the landscape that has been given and find a way to best tend the field with the tools you have immediately around you; for all we are given is the present moment and the future untold. The past should be used to learn from (in hindsight), to make amends, and to demonstrate progress in moving forward. But when the aim of the resolution is to serve a single ego only, the landscape has already become poisoned. And that was the landscape we were always found to be standing upon, both guilty in some regard.

Spiritual Miscues

Though it took me until years after my marriage ended to understand where the underpinnings to our foundation first came unglued, I would go on to learn that understanding how to be a counterweight to Love involved much more than even words or actions alone. Being a counterweight would prove to be most importantly based on each of our own spiritual journeys. Unto each person in a relationship, there must be an equal amount of willingness to maintain peace and harmony. Sometimes one side bends more than the other, but that can be expected. It is within the extremes that the dissonance begins to occur. And like a pipe that gains a small leak, the inevitable burst will occur if the leak is not properly mended. A patched hole can only bide time. So when a person is still searching for his own salvation – his own peace within himself and in his Creator – the greatest exertion of energy to maintain a relationship will never be enough. I have to believe that while each of us may not have recognized it at the time, our own personal walks were affecting the potential for what could have been.

Before my marriage, I was once grounded in faith in ways greater than I could ever seek to explain at that time. As a child, I wanted to be baptized on Christmas morning. Just as I knew that Jesus gave His life for us in a way that mankind could understand at that time, I wanted to give my life to all that He represented on the day we celebrated his birth. It was the greatest gift I could give – and all of this from the mind of a child. But, somehow, during the course of our marriage, my spiritual compass had lost its bearings. It wasn't that I had managed to lose my spirituality. In fact, we continued trying multiple churches and bringing God into our lives with greater effort than in the beginning. But, it was in the way I allowed my body, mind and soul to lose the balance they once retained – the gravity created among the three that enables life to be and holds us together in harmony with All That Is. The collective effort we made to bring God back into our lives should make it apparent enough in the action of the effort itself to understand the problem – for God is always there, and any attempt to "bring him into your life" indicates that the relationship with Him is already misunderstood. For us, we were forcing a solution onto something that only needed uncovered, thus complicating the issue even more.

    Naively unaware to the spiritual miscues, I sought to understand why Stacey seemed insolvably unhappy with me. I allowed ego to take control as "I" focused on what "I" could do to help her find happiness. With blame falling on neither party, over the years it had become clear that she was unsatisfied in our marriage – so much so that she would tell me indirectly in the kindest words possible; all filled with hope for a better day. I could tell it broke her heart to say any words that indicated unhappiness – and perhaps that is why it never quite registered that she was falling out of Love with me. She always wanted to find a way to be happy and desired happiness for us together, but her personal unhappiness was becoming too insurmountable for her to keep moving on without change. Every attempt I made to bring happiness unto her was met with an equal amount of repulsion. The greater the effort, the greater we became divided. If I had only known that these were the signs to the beginning of the end, I probably would have sought to protect my heart. But instead, I drove blindly ahead thinking this was just a bump on the road of our perceived fairytale life. I never thought that I would be in a marriage that ended in divorce. It wasn't even a possibility. For all intents and purposes, my heart was still madly in Love with her, and I held to the belief that she still Loved me – and perhaps she really did.

Indeed, the more I have thought about the contributors to her sadness, the more I have realized that they were not truly unsolvable. They only appeared unsolvable at the time because of a lack of understanding of the true root of the problem…that root being each of our own personal walk's with God. But through our conversations, I turned away from His guidance and tried to take control of the situation. I decided that the solution was to make more money, because money seemed to always be an issue in our marriage. Even if the goal was to reach financial freedom so we could one day be happy and free from financial stress, the goal was misguided because it attempted to control how we provided for ourselves instead of placing faith in the opportunities that God desired to put in our lives in order to provide for our well being.

There always seemed to be a newer car that we needed or a bigger house. During our five years of marriage we went through the purchases of five new cars and three new homes, countless big ticket items – none of which ever seemed to fulfill the chasm between us. My job allowed for Stacey to be a housewife and an eventual stay-at-home mom while still allowing for us live a quality lifestyle. However, it never quite seemed to be enough for either of us. Though I experienced a fair amount of financial success early in my twenties, I did not enjoy my job. I hoarded the unhappiness away within the depths of my soul. I perceived it to be a necessary part of my life to help her be happy. My happiness fell second to hers. But when her happiness went unresolved, it meant that I, too, had a seemingly insurmountable amount of unhappiness buried within the depths of my soul – though never was any of it related to my Love for her.

In the final days of our marriage, we had still never spent a night apart from each other (going all of the way back to before we were engaged). We always slept in the same bed – every night…possibly on either side of the bed, but it was the same bed either way. There was never a moment where one of us visited friends or family without the other. Whether or not that was the best thing for a marriage, it is hard to say. But for us, we were trying. The harmony our souls held with each other fought the good fight. We tried under every circumstance to make our marriage work. And though I did not ever expect that our marriage would end in any other way than upon each of us taking our last breaths in old age together, there came a weekend in July that we would spend our first night apart and inevitably our last night together.

She Said Goodbye

I was twenty-seven and had just received a promotion to the senior management team at my place of work. It occurred right about the same time of the year when the executive team travelled to a retreat in the mountains for professional growth and leisure. It would be the first business retreat of my career and also the first time during our marriage that Stacey and I would spend a night apart. In the nearly seven years we had known each other, the strength we found in our proximity now had the opportunity to find weakness. And, if weakness was intending to seep in and compromise our marriage, it had found its chance.

Since this would be the first time spent apart from each other, Stacey wanted to travel to her parent's house several hours away and stay the weekend with them. Without a second thought, I supported her. It was a great opportunity for her family to see our young daughter and help Stacey care for her as well. So, that weekend she took our daughter down to her family's house in Georgia. Upon my return from the retreat, I had expected her to have already arrived at the house before me (based on our previous night's conversation). But when I arrived, she was not there. She called not long after my arrival and told me she wanted to spend a few extra days at

Gravity Calling

her parent's house. My heart sank, but I never let her know it while we were on the phone. Even up until that phone call, I had zero expectation that anything would ever draw us permanently apart. But this call was different. I could tell her demeanor had changed. While the recent weeks had been much tougher for us than most, this was the first time I ever had any idea that something was un-fixably wrong. My soul knew it when I heard her voice. My mind denied it in her words. My heart would know it a couple days later. But in that moment, I just smiled and encouraged her to enjoy the time with her family.

A couple of days later when she returned home, she greeted me with the cliché "we need to talk." I sat in the floor of the large hallway of our old, historic home leaning against the wall. I knew this was the end. She went on to tell me everything my soul already had identified in the phone call and that my mind had tried to deny in her words. She told me that she wanted a trial separation. While I can't imagine "remaining collected" would ever apply to anyone in that situation, I did my best to resemble those terms. On the inside I was crumbling. On the outside, I was crying. But in my words, I held strength. I asked for counseling, or for anything that could possibly prevent the end, but we both knew those were not solutions. A hard line had been drawn in the sand. This was it. There would be no "trial" in the separation – only a finite ending. With never a night spent apart until that weekend, we would never spend another night together again.

She Said Goodbye

We separated that evening and just a few months later, were divorced without lawyer involvement as amicably as anyone could ever hope to be. Even the morning that she said goodbye, we stayed up all night and talked about who each other should date, what we should look for, how to be better for the next person, and just generally how to move forward with our lives. I imagine I needed to hear it more than her. It was now apparent that she had been planning the end and I was just now privy to the content of this chapter. But if there was ever a way to part ways, I would not have wanted to do it in any other way than we did that morning. I would not be who I am today, nor would she grow into who she is today if we had taken different roads. Most importantly, neither of us would have the relationship we have with our daughter – who is the single greatest thing that has ever happened to either of us. Though the ending came with heartbreak and the seemingly insurmountable heartache in the years following, I would never have done anything differently. I will always hold hope that someday, someone else will come along and hear the song of Stacey's soul and see just how beautiful it is. She deserves every bit of that.

Scattered Pieces

Broken. It is the only word I can use to describe myself in the aftermath of that unsuspecting July evening. I was now just pieces of a man I once was before. And if for a moment, imagine all of those pieces of my life shattered across the floor around me – every piece was so bittersweet. Everyday I pulled myself out of bed, placed my bare feet on the floor, and walked across the broken pieces of a life that now seemed to lack meaning, lack purpose, lack hope; each broken piece inherently slicing deeply into each foot with every step I took as I walked across the floor and prepared myself to begin each day. This is just how it was. Nothing would be different for years to come, though I would learn to mask the pain from everyone around me. It was a lesson in learning how to deal with an inconceivable reality until the remnants of my previous life managed to fade into the distance or someone else managed to defy the odds and cause my compass to find true north again.

These shattered pieces were all that remained from the ending to an otherwise fairytale life. To say I was blindsided would be an understatement of the greatest magnitude. And, "broken" barely describes the feeling I felt within my soul. It would be like removing music or art from someone's life – a song that has been playing in the forefront of their life for seven years and having only silence remain; a void absent of beauty, of certainty, of safety, calm and peace. There are reasons why music is said to soothe the soul and why a restless baby will fall asleep to a brilliant symphony or lullaby. And even if the song my soul had played in the company of hers for the past seven years contained some dissonant notes, some missteps and offbeat tempos, the song was a beautiful imperfection.

As I learned to walk again in absence of song, I buried myself in work, social life, and friends. I chased every dream I had ever longed to do in a mad rush trying to save my soul from crashing to the ground. The faster I moved, the more I could do. And the more I could do, the less chance my soul had at bottoming out on the ground. So I moved. I moved at speeds blinding to those around me. My life became a mad wash of exuberant activities. My career excelled at breakneck speeds. My social life went from zero to "I must know everybody" in no time flat. I decided it was a great time to experience the first beer in my life. That beer led to wine, liquor and cigars. I became a connoisseur of fine wines and cigars from around the world. I learned to chat it up about yachts and dreams of sailing around the world to those I shared in conversation over wine and cigars. It's important to note that at the time of this writing, I still have never been on a sailboat, but that didn't stop me from talking about my dreams.

It seemed I spent more weekends at the beach than in the land-locked state where I lived. I travelled the country to places I had never been. I went to Vegas and learned how to

Scattered Pieces

gamble...and ultimately how not to gamble. I dated. Actually, I did not date – I had "extreme dates" wherein I'd invite a girl out on a Saturday not telling her what it was we were going to do. Then, I'd surprise her with a grand date of epic proportions – an over abundance of demonstration to offset my own hurt. Every date had to consist of something I had never done. I went hang gliding. I went on hot-air balloon rides. I went on evening dinner cruises – each date ending without me even attempting to kiss the girl or show any intimacy. Every date was meant to be a shimmer of amazing wrapped up in brevity, and never a second call back. Though the girls I took out were all potentially amazing, it was more important for me to leave them at the end of the date with a story they could tell for years to come. I wanted to leave happiness. If anything, I was painting the world in the colors of my heart, leaving a mark in a way only I could. In my pain, there would be happiness for others.

The friends I made, drew together in a way that only the craze of emotions and lifestyle I was experiencing could do at the time. Summers on the lake, winters at the beach, concerts every weekend, sporting events every evening. Maybe it was a colossal explosion of people uniting under similar circumstances, but the group of around forty people (whom I did not know prior to my divorce, nor did most of them know each other) spent the first years of my suffering acting like family – all drawn together and held close when I was around. There was rarely a day that a large portion of us were not spending time together. Maybe they saw a soul crushed and hurting and their own souls cried out in sympathy. Maybe it was divine timing. But sometimes I like to think that the world is purely what we make of it. And though I was making blunders and mistakes faster than I had ever made in my life, I was attempting to paint the world in happiness with those around me serving as the pigments of color – all helping me create something beautiful that brought light unto the darkness I felt within. The world was my canvas, the people my colors, the motion and events of my actions were the strokes of brilliance and blunders placed upon the world around me.

    I wrote. I wrote and recorded more songs than I had ever written in my life. The rush of emotions was more than I had ever experienced and I had to learn how to channel each and every feeling. Each person I met inspired something new within me. It wasn't as if I thought I was falling in Love each time – far from it. But, I was observing people's intricacies – the little things that make each person unique. Maybe it was something spoken in conversation. Maybe it was a peculiar mannerism. Maybe it was just the glow of life housed within them that radiated a slightly different shade and combination of hues than the next. Everything around me was saturated in inspiration that helped me keep moving – that helped keep me from crashing to the ground.

    Though I tried to move forward, the truth is that it was only a smile and a beer that held the pain at bay. Inevitably I would have to return home at the end of each evening, driving forty minutes away from all signs of life in the city. This was the house that Stacey wanted and the last place I wanted to

Scattered Pieces

return. It is likely the hardest thing I ever did at the end of each day – to walk through a house with memories built together, seeing the pictures of a life that once was, the remaining furniture that was picked out together, the places we would sit when I arrived home. I tried my best to avoid returning home. I kept an overnight bag in my Jeep and a change of clothes in my office so I could try to sleep somewhere else anytime I was gone. But even my best efforts could not avoid the past permanently. Through it all, there is only one thing I could have done differently, but never chose to do to help ease this burden. Instead, I chose to ignore God.

Stained Glass

For something to be perfect, it must have once been broken – perhaps twice broken. Because it is within all of the imperfections and broken pieces that beauty is created. I used to think perfection was in the flawless – the perfect job with no stress; the perfect physique with no work; the perfect clarity of diamond; the perfect fairytale life with no pain. But now I've come to realize that perfection is in the flawed. For if everyone and everything, every circumstance, and every need were never to have any flaws, we would be unable to discern true beauty, perfection, and the rare.

The rare are those that stand alone – separating themselves from their very surroundings and people in their lives without anyone ever noticing the separation. They blend in to the present, architected by their past. These are the people who have experienced hurt, experienced pain. These are the people who have made mistakes and have been judged harshly for something in their past or even in their present. But despite the judgments, the endured hurt and pain, these are the people who have begun to put the pieces of their lives back together – a medley of broken shards of glass now held together in strength, certainty, and – most importantly – by faith.

Gravity Calling

The broken shards of glass form a picture of past experiences, past hurts, past rebuilds, breaks, and rebuilds again. If a person is to be seen as having the light of their soul illuminating the fragile body in which it is housed, the broken will always stand out. The unbroken have little imperfection allowing most of the light to naively pass through their body in a single burst of radiance. But the broken are beautifully flawed. Like a stained glass window in a Victorian chapel, the pieces of shattered glass that once represented their lives – pieces once broken on the floor around them – have been put back together in such a way that a new story is told. Though I've never been told such, I can only imagine the stained glass windows housed within churches must represent this very same concept. How better to share a spiritual story than through broken pieces of glass, bound together, with light shining through? And even then, the true beauty of stained glass is only revealed when light-on-fire ignites the tones and colors of the glass, casting a bath of rainbow colors into the room. That is how I see perfection: a beautiful rainbow of colors cast in a bath of light from the soul, through the shards of broken glass that represent the pieces of a life that once was and what it has now become.

As I began to slowly but surely rebuild my life, I realized it was akin to trying to find a way to put the shattered pieces back together. Along the way I realized I would never be the same again. The puzzle pieces were shattered beyond recognition of what once was, preventing me from rebuilding myself as I was before. But perhaps this time, I would be stronger;

Stained Glass

Love harder; enjoy life just a little more; and showcase a brilliance of spirit radiating from my soul. For this time, the pieces would not be bound by their mass alone, protected in their fragility. This time, each shard would be held together by sustenance; by experience – strong and flexible in function. Even if the structure were to crack or crumble again, it would only occur in small pieces falling to the floor which could more easily be picked back up and put together again.

The pieces of my life slowly began to be reassembled over time. Though I tried to ignore the past in order to keep the pain at bay, I found that if I could find one small opportunity each day to pick up just one of the tiny shards of my shattered life and find a place for it in the great stained glass portrait my soul would one day become, then I could consider the painful breaths I breathed in to be worth the oxygen I consumed. The puzzle came together slowly, but not for lack of trying. I found that I was working without a finished image to strive to create; no blueprint in form or design. The stained glass was an evolving piece of art wherein the image created needed to have form, clarity, strength, life, passion, and truth. It needed to house beauty, experience, Love, trust, and be founded on the principal of faith. And somehow in the end, it needed to represent who I was and who I would become. But faith had become hard to rationalize in my life. It wasn't that I had lost track of God. It was more like I placed Him on hold every time He called, hoping He would hang up and call back at a later time. I wasn't quite ready for His intervention. The happiness I was trying to paint on the canvas of the world around me required me to stray from my walk with Him; I was caught somewhere between blah and uncertainty trying to find my way home. And there would be no way that I could fully put the pieces of my life back together without understanding faith as the keystone.

So I built. I rebuilt. I created art and would subsequently tear it down. Every design never seemed quite right; every design was inherently flawed and incomplete. With every experience and every circumstance, I would find reason to rebuild what I thought the end form of the stained glass should resemble. But every time it was incomplete. How I could recreate the most ideal form possible was always the nagging question on my mind. The all-consuming thought of my existence, purpose, and intention on this Earth always seemed unresolved. Over the years, I rebuilt the stained-glass to my soul as best as possible – weighing on circumstances past and experiences future. In the present I found resolve in the structure I had created. Though it took nearly three years of design, I had managed to rebuild and reshape what once was into something I felt would be able to endure the test of time.

Yet it was still missing something – something I had yet to identify. On the outside, the structure was beautifully broken and attentively mended. But it was missing the fire – the light that once resided within. For every bit of patience and care I took to rebuild the outer structure, I also chose to encase my soul in a granite shell – impenetrable to anyone who would try to take a peek. This granite shell was to serve as my protection, my guard against being broken again. To me at the time, I

Stained Glass

viewed self-protection as a boundary separating my soul from the outer world. But the funny thing about that granite shell, is that it encased the light within. And if I could explain the beauty in stained glass again, it is the fire-alive igniting the hues, colors, and refractions of light from the broken shards of what once was. Stained glass alone is just a picture, a story to be told. But light shining through stained glass is radiance blessed, a spiritual song in wonder to the rare that has been found within.

Return To Genesis

My protection was a demonstration in self-preservation; a defiance of faith. True protection should have been found in the burning light of a rekindled soul shining through a rebuilt exterior, telling my stained glass story to those desiring to listen. But it would take more growth on my journey to understand that light is the only protection we have, and the granite casing was merely a misdirection – a prison from all that could be. I was misguiding myself by misplacing faith during the times of my life's uncertainty.

Nearly three years of rebuilding led me to an unfamiliar destination. For every step forward I considered taking, my spirit was already taking two steps back. I suppose if there is an irony to it all, it would be that my spirit was racing backwards to the beginning faster than I could move forward to the destination without faith in tow. My rebuilt stained glass frame, was merely that – a frame unlit from the inside and shielded from light passing into its core from the outside. My viewpoint prohibited me from seeing the very structure that had been rebuilt despite the quality, care, and craftsmanship permeating the design. It was as if I blindly built something I did not allow myself to see, though was guided to create from the very depths of my soul.

Gravity Calling

As much as I believed I was returning to the world in whole form and stability, my spirit was running as fast as it could to help me find redirection in the error of my ways. I was blind and oblivious to my misdirection. Perhaps there was just one grand moment that spoke to my soul like a giant white flag waving, begging the surrender of my soul – but that moment will be the center point of something more special in the pages to come. For now, as I returned to the world ready to face better days, I forged onward into uncharted waters looking for any land where I could step foot onto the shore. My journey led me to the shores of the entrepreneurial world – a step onto a shore of an island jungle that eventually led me scourging into the depths of darkness, looking for any sense of light to lead me back home. If there was ever a flicker, a glint, a glimmer of hope that my soul would shine through the granite casing in those final days of my entrepreneurial endeavors, the final circumstances extinguished any and all sense of hope within. A series of unfortunate circumstances, grand miscues, and Divine design – it was days before my thirtieth birthday, and my soul had found its way back to the starting line; the origin of my Genesis.

Starting Lines & Picket Lines

Ahead were the moments that sent me on an expedition to dig deep within my existence and salvage any sense of optimism and wonder I once had remaining in my life. These were the days I searched for hope. These were the days I searched for purpose. These were the days I searched for reason to be – reaching for anything to help me gather my bearings and find understanding in the darkness that had encumbered me so.

What does a starting line look like for someone who has never stepped foot in a race? Is it the staggered starting points around a track that a runner envisions? Is it the markings on the asphalt of a speedway? Is it just a timer on a stopwatch that is activated with a certain movement? Is it the sound of a horn or gunshot signifying it is time? During our time here on Earth, I would say there is not one single point or definition of a starting line, for everyone is standing on the starting line for their journey – whether they realize it or not, or even if they have chosen to accept this simple truth. But as I stood in the darkness, I was in denial that the darkness was a starting line. I saw it as a crash-and-burn ending to everything that could have been. Only in the climb out of darkness would I see that I was right where I needed to be. In God's eyes, I had found my way to the starting line. And, like a father who has to watch his child fall in order to get back up, this was the time God helped me learn to see, find the light within, and understand the journey through His undying Love.

    I would come to learn that life is a series of starting lines and picket lines. There are no finish lines – only the recognition of crossing new starting lines, slightly changing the objective and course from where you once were. You can choose to stop and stand in defiance – picketing the next part of the journey; and many people do so without ever recognizing their actions join the crowd of picketers – even if their voice would indicate otherwise. Or you can continue forward, putting one foot in front of the other, feeling out the path that lies ahead. There is nothing wrong with being safe. There is nothing wrong with feeling out the path before running head first into the darkness. For it is only in hindsight a person can turn around and view the blazing trail left behind, illuminating the once darkened path and providing hope for others in proximity. My eyes were only truly opened in the darkness – the depths of the suffocating blackness I found myself in the week heading into my thirtieth birthday. As many jokes as are made about turning thirty years old, I was standing in the middle of a collision of circumstances I never saw coming. I was sideswiped by a barrage of artifacts that I had undoubtedly created for myself, though I was oblivious to having created them along the way, and even more oblivious to the impending crash of epic proportions that would occur in one sweeping moment.

My race into the darkness began when I had suddenly found myself no longer with any income and only a few days shy from having nothing in my bank account – every single bill waiting ahead in resilience. And while that description of my financial struggle seems inappropriately insignificant to call "darkness," it is important to understand that at that time – money was my spirit. It was an endless opportunity of fun, friends, and escape from the heartache I was still experiencing from my divorce. Money was the fuel to my life. My career produced money. My ego took charge believing it produced the very fuel used to ward off the demons and negative feelings in the aftermath of my divorce two years prior. Without it, I did not know how to live – how to be. When I became finically siphoned off from the world, the lights went out. This was the beginning of darkness – the point before blackness finds its darkest point from the afterglow of what once was. To another, darkness could arrive in another way. For me, this is the method God chose to teach me to see.

Everything I had come to know in the wake of my divorce increasingly hinged upon my financial ability to bring superficial happiness into my life. The people that surrounded me in that time of pain boarded my train and enjoyed the ride and accommodations I set forth. I rarely found myself in Nashville, and when I did, my life became one superfluous free-for-all with the money I made. Never would I have considered myself

Gravity Calling

wealthy – careless, yes – but, for my age and outgoing expenses, I had an egregious amount of extra income I could use to medicate my feelings. I built a life upon a house of cards. It was forged out of what I considered financial necessities during my marriage: a large mortgage, two car notes, a business credit card, and all expenses floated monthly (but paid off in full) across personal credit cards with excessive limits. But the day I found myself with no income after losing the financial backer to my entrepreneurial endeavors, and days from bottoming out my bank account, I panicked. There was no money to pay off the large monthly expenses floated on credit cards; no way to pay the upcoming house payment; no way to pay for anything. The financial house of cards I had built my life upon was about to fall. And all it would take was the slightest breeze to blow the first card over.

In the wake of my impending financial collapse, my ego was crushed – and rightly so. The arrogance in believing the world around me was everything "I" had created was possibly one of my greatest misinterpretations of all. To my ego, perception was everything; it was the very foundation on which my recovery from my divorce had been built upon. So when facing the impending collapse of the materialistic world I had built around myself, I would search everywhere to find a victim to blame for my financial collapse. Every person held fault within my eyes. That is, everyone but me. Pride – ego's best friend – prevented me from seeing, prevented me from seeking God, and prevented me from identifying the ways I could enable myself to recover. Though I faced the all important challenge of damage control and recovery, I would eventually find myself facing foreclosure, battling a newly accrued debt north of fifty thousand dollars, two upside-down car notes, refacing the sadness created in the wake of my divorce, the struggle to pay child support and see my daughter due to financial constraints, and most importantly the absence of Love – all while resisting employment opportunities that seemed beneath me as pride continued to take charge in those decisions. I had exhausted my retirement accounts, sold my stock, and cashed in other investments that had yet to pay off just to survive. It was a beautiful disaster of rampant financial carelessness; one that I needed to experience.

 The financial chaos took a beating to my ego, though it fought a strong fight. My ego led me down paths of poor-me-pity-parties, indulging in selfish and careless acts, eventually finding myself in a tragic comedy of coin-toss legal battles that I had convinced myself were defined by the gray – not the black and white. I pushed away the people that had once been an important part of my life; in fact, they were the pillars of the life I had created. And though I believed that no one was there for me when I needed it the most – even if I just needed someone to listen to me and hear me talk – perhaps the most eye-opening moment came when I realized they were never there to begin with. They were products of my ego; products that could only have been present when my ego was around, standing strong while suppressing my spirit. In the wake of the fight the financial struggle was taking to my ego, no one wanted to be around. They only wanted to be around a winner – a victor. The ego knows nothing about losing, so anyone who falters or is caught up in a fight is immediately left curbside and disbanded from the products it once created. Ego has no mercy regardless if it is the created or the creator. It plays by an entirely different set of rules than the spirit.

How I had gotten here and landed in this moment of uncertainty is the question that would mark my starting line – the question wherein I would have to uncover my very first misstep, the root cause buried beneath the egoic rubble that represented only the symptoms of all that it was covering. So I began to run. In the darkness I ran. Carelessly, clumsily bouncing off of objects in the pitch black while my eyes took time to adjust, searching for anything that could be perceived as a pinhole of light – a moment of hope to guide me home. That moment would eventually come by way of a very important decision I felt impressed to make on a day six months after I first found myself in the darkness – a decision that forever changed my life. And from that decision forward, over the course of the next three years, the darkness would begin to subside, giving way to light – a light brilliant in luster, a light of the brightest white. As the light would seep in, it would begin to illuminate the track I was running upon. The signs I would come to see during my race were markers indicating each next required step on the journey into the light. Though I would not necessarily understand the words as they appeared on the signs, all I could do was keep running the race. The signs would read:

...

"Life, Loss, & Love – and the greatest of these is Love. From heretofore the experience of each shall occur bound by the veil, and the veil removed."

...

Despite my inability to understand the words, all arrows pointed straight ahead. Any missteps were only points of redirection helping me navigate through the pitch black caverns of self-discovery and into the light.

Kindred Souls

There are souls, spiritual brethren that have been placed within proximity of each of us to help us along the journey. I like to believe that my soul and these brethren made a pact, a promise, long before we came to experience life on Earth that we would be there for each other in times of need. Though each of us would have to fumble our way through the veil of our existence, rediscovering our soul on the journey – whenever each of us came to a point in recognition of All That Was, we would be there, ready to help our kindred souls along the journey.

As I was lost in the darkness, I made a very important decision six months along the journey to pick up the phone and call my cousin Bryan. Perhaps I thought I had exhausted all of my other immediate friends and needed to borrow a new ear – one unswayed from knowledge of my encumbered darkness. However, as I came to realize, the impetus behind the call was not an egoic need to plead my case and receive justification of my misery in another. It was my soul crying out for help to a spiritual brethren, a kindred soul. Bryan and I had not spoken to each other in over ten years leading into that conversation. Though he is my first cousin and we were extremely close as children, our lives had taken us separate ways during each of our marriages. And while I would not know it in the beginning of our calls, he too was experiencing a similar situation with his marriage of seventeen years. The call was one of divine timing, and one that I can't help but look back and realize as the single most important call to action that my soul took during the days of my darkness.

During the call, our conversation bounced around between a variety of topics and somehow found itself drifting into the topic of dreams. I asked Bryan what he thought about dreams and if he had ever tried to induce dreams or explore the science behind them. It may have seemed like a random topic for discussion, but it fell into the context of our original conversation. It also seemed as if it would be entertaining and fun to toss around harmless ideas about the topic as well. He shared with me about how he tried exploring dreams as a teenager, but after a few experiences that he was uncharacteristically vague in explaining, decided to not explore them any further. He also had chosen to avoid meditation for a similar reason. Of course this piqued my curiosity. Now I had just been given reason to explore the unknown. After our call ended, I tried meditating for the first time in my life. I had no idea what I was doing – or even if I was doing it right. I had no form of guidance or reference points to know what to even look for. Though my mind was dead-set on believing the inexplicable was explainable through science, the experiences in the moments following the call kick-started a journey out of Genesis and into the days of wandering through my Exodus, eventually helping me find God again. It was an accidental

Kindred Souls

happenchance of conversational topics with Bryan that went on to demonstrate God's grand design.

While the details are not important in the experience I had in the moments following our call, I can say that while attempting to meditate, God opened my eyes. With my physical eyes closed, He allowed me to experience a moment preceding my birth – one that involved my grandparents. This was the third "vision" I had ever experienced – one so clear, so vivid. In my childhood I had experienced two distinct visions that revealed the events of the following day, before they occurred. I came to learn in our conversation that Bryan, too, had experienced similar phenomena. In fact, I'd guess most people have experienced at least one unexplainable dream or vision in their life, but few even rarely talk about it for fear of being judged. But outside of those two events, I had not experienced any real dreams or visions up until this point in my life.

Immediately after the vision occurred, I called Bryan back. I explained to him what I had been shown in my vision concerning our grandparents. He immediately became extremely excited and shared with me a photo that had been passed down from our grandparents to his father, and then to him that captured an image of my vision with extreme precision. I had never seen the photo, nor would I have. Bryan had only received it upon his father's passing – and only one picture existed from that time period of our grandparent's lives. It had been given to his father as a child and had been stuffed away in a shoe box for decades. This was the first moment that

Gravity Calling

Bryan and I shared a call-and-response type of divine handshake – one that would continue to happen to this day (we would later come to call these seven-and-seven moments, which will be explained at a later point in this book). From this point forward, Bryan decided he would embark with me on a journey in understanding visions and dreams. At this point, the journey wasn't a quest in searching for God – He wasn't even part of the equation in our minds yet. This was a moment of simply exploring the unknown.

As we embarked on the journey, I chose science as my stallion. I created numerous tools and methods that helped me align my mind and body with more precision in an attempt to invoke and experience visions like I had that first evening when I hung up the phone with Bryan. I researched every topic that I could get my hands on. I read every historic philosophical, theological and ancient document I could find. It even led me to learning the underpinnings of Hebrew and Greek to better understand the original context behind some of the oldest documents known to mankind. With each nugget of information learned, I increasingly realized that the modern contributions of science only provided higher precision tools to help the mind, body and soul find its center – a center that was much more understood by a mankind that was unencumbered by the distractions of modern life. Splinters of that knowledge can be found across the globe in forms of meditation, martial arts, dancing, yoga, silence of the monks, prayer, fasting, religion, and art.

I eventually realized the stallion I was riding was no longer needed to make the journey. I could do so by hand and by foot with more grace and mobility than the stallion could offer. Perhaps in the beginning, I needed something to carry me through the initial steps of learning how to calm my mind and body – something that I could hold onto for security in finding a future point of resolve. Never did I think that the irrational would become the only rationality that I would ever need and would forevermore permeate my existence. Though my race would take approximately a year before I would begin to wean myself from science to find unconfined communion with God, it was my set of training wheels. I used the knowledge I had around me, the understanding of a mashup of Eastern and Western philosophies, and all available means of philosophical knowledge from our most ancient ancestors to understand dreams and visions. In the beginning, I thought I was journeying down the path of dreams and meditation as an outlet for my creative energies during the days of my darkness. It would eventually turn out that I was exploring the very concept that God would use to begin to speak to me.

...

The Prestige

That first phone call with Bryan led to a call every week or two. Some of these would last for a couple of minutes, some would run into the hours. Over the years, those calls would stretch to three or four calls a week, an hour or two at a time.

Gravity Calling

With each call we would talk about the dreams we were having. We each worked on practicing meditation in an effort to improve the stillness in our minds. As we dedicated every moment outside of work to this concept, our levels of awareness increased. Dreams would begin to occur more frequently, more vividly. Meditation would begin to reveal more in the stillness than I would ever have expected (or even thought to believe through other people's written words). I had preconceived notions of what I believed to be truths instead of searching out and defining truths myself. In stillness, sensations such as vibrations throughout the spine and the feeling of chakras spinning in vortex-like motions began to occur. Eventually the understanding of how the mind interprets these sensations in a visual form began to occur. Through these experiences, we came to understand that these sensations occur constantly to everyone in the human experience, but the noise of the outside world distracts most from noticing. With each day, our bodily recognition in energies became stronger, music as a divinely architected language became revealed, geometry in motion found reason, and the symbiotic balance found in life brought an unquantifiable amount of clarity to the world around us. Approximately three months into our calls, something remarkable happened. Bryan and I shared a vision.

When Bryan and I began discussing the vision, it was all we could do to not assume we were messing with each other. As he began to explain his vision and I recognized he was sharing the same vision I had just experienced the night before, I would stop him and fill in the pieces. He'd pick up where I left off. This continued throughout the explanation of the vision. It was the moment we would never again question each other; the moment we knew there was something greater working in our lives. It would go on to be the first of more visions to come where we shared experiences, or shared altered perceptions of the same scenario. I have to believe that through our unyielding dedication to uncovering answers to dreams and visions, God again gave us a new starting line. This time, the line showed us interconnectivity, which would inevitably lead to finding Him.

We would also come to realize, even in the early stages of the journey, that it takes two souls for the journey to be made so that experiences are not easily dismissed. For if one person goes at it alone, the inexplicable is easily dismissible. But those who journey in the comfort of another of equal trust, light, and faith – someone they can grow with together and speak with no fear of judgment – the inexplicable gains a foundation; a form of verification to the mind that it is indeed experiencing something greater than is rationalized from science alone. From that point forward, we began to realize we were venturing onto a spiritual path, though I tried to bring science in tow. We began to recognize that we had been purposed for each other to experience this portion of the journey together all along. We even began to recognize that we knew each other as spiritual brethren as early as our childhoods (even if it was more of an unknown feeling of recognition in another at the time). There were certain conversations we had as children that had echoes in the beginnings of our spiritual journeys together – and were found in that first shared vision.

Over the first year of the journey, the number of visions increased in frequency from one every few months to at least one a month. At this point, we still continued to divide the concepts of dreams and visions into two separate categories of things that could happen in the mind during sleep or meditation. But when the visions began to enter into this rate of frequency and our understanding grew in their significance, the divide of dreams and visions began to give way to an understanding of the two concepts as one. And nearly as quickly as those two concepts began to merge, spiritual experiences began to occur where we directly communed with the same Great Angels that are written about in the Bible, and some angels who gave us names that were unheard of until we would research the depths of the internet and happen across old ancient texts that documented these lesser known angels names and experiences. We would also each experience direct communions with God, Our Creator – experiences of which are so overpowering that they are a constant source of weeping when explaining the experience to another.

In the second year, the visions and spiritual experiences progressed in strength and frequency and were occurring at least once a week, with much greater clarity and sensation. Even the divide between how we classified visions and spiritual experiences began to merge. Now into my third year – as I approach the age of 33, I can firmly say that when I close my eyes, my soul is no longer bound by my body. I do not sleep. I find peace in meditation before my body falls asleep – conditioning my body and ego to release my soul from its confines. Every single night I experience memorable experiences in the heavens. Every wakened meditation, my soul is allowed to traverse the heavens. Every night I learn something new that I bring back to Earth that helps me interpret the world around me. I have written about these experiences in six other books including my personal journal, which is appropriately entitled Rebirth. For it will eventually be seen that the three years from age 30 to 33 were the years of my soul's rebirth – a spiritual awakening inside. It became a time where I no longer identified myself as a body, but rather a soul. Accompanied on Earth by the most spiritual brother I have ever known in Bryan, during these three years I journeyed from the darkness into the light. And while the details of my journey can be seen to some as relevant on a micro level, this book is about the macro – a view from above, which is why the other six books are not included in this context. There are, however, a handful of experiences that I have included in this book to help guide the reader through the story.

Eventually Bryan and I came to the understanding that we are all children of God on a divine playground – the playground being how we experience life, and the way God communicates with us. Younger children are just happy to be anywhere with their parents, content to play in whatever space is within a safe arm's reach. Others begin to understand that the playground holds new adventures that they desire to experience. These children will run to the merry-go-round and

Gravity Calling

enjoy the feeling of spinning until they cannot walk straight. Then they will run over to the swing-set and attempt to defy gravity, soaring higher and higher with each swing. At some point, a child becomes aware that the playground is bound by a fence and wants to leave its bounds. At that point, the child will meet some form of a gatekeeper – someone or something making sure that the children stay on the playground.

It is at this point in the metaphor of spiritual recognition, that the playground parallels adulthood in our earthly walk – and the understanding of dreams being no more than mindless thoughts, despite however religious someone may claim to be. But as a child begins to wonder about what else exists outside of the fence of the playground, he begins to move around and observe older kids playing games on a field some distance away, outside the gates. The child begins dreaming of playing these games with the big kids and tells his friends about it. It remains a myth to those children unable to see, a story of fantasy and intrigue to others, and a story that leads some children to the edge of the fence to see for themselves the older kids playing in the distance. Some children will find their way to the gate. But only when a child has demonstrated the most dedicated growth and commitment on his spiritual journey and willingness to humble himself as a student with no knowledge of truth, will the child be escorted outside the gates and begin to enjoy the view. Even then, the child is still unaware there are even greater truths beyond the field in view.

The moment of being escorted from the playground is where the greatest spiritual experiences begin to occur. This is the time when spiritual understanding becomes some hybrid of a choose-your-own-adventure book and an ambiguous mystery novel where it is up to the reader to decide what the author intended to mean. If the events were to be written in black and white, the human experience would not be required. This is why it is important to share the journey with another. Truths become what are learned through the experiences gleaned, and through the nonjudgmental and non-biased conversations that occur when the events are recounted to each other. Each person should have complete trust in the other that nothing said will ever be looked upon as anything other than a child seeing the world for the very first time, with no preconceived notions of how to interpret it, or even what it yet means. For the only rules ever given for mankind to abide by were the Ten Commandments. No other religion, no other prophet, no other source of divine knowledge conflicts with this simple truth. Everything else is just conjecture or spiritual guideposts, for there are no wrongs outside of the moral rules God set forth to us – only the decision to move forward and take each experience as it is presented, to learn, to grow...and eventually find the destination and the purpose in the earthly walk. The moments of being escorted from the playground are the moments of communion with the angels – moments that sound like fantasy until it actually occurs. Within each person, the opportunity to experience this amazing part of the journey exists, only to be revealed as the veil of ego begins to be removed.

...

Walking By Faith

From a child playing on a playground through the growth of beginning to understand how God works in our earthly lives, we are each tasked with learning to understand how God communicates with each of us. For each person, it will be a little different – in a way tailored specifically for each person to understand with respect to his place along the journey. Just as we speak to a child in simple terms so he can learn to understand, so too does God begin with simple methods for us to take notice. A person would never read a doctoral thesis to a child and expect him to understand what is being said – especially if that child is just learning how to say "mama" and "dada." It is often the point of confusion among others because as we grow in our earthly life, we are taught that the world is quantifiable, and that results are reproducible – that we already know the basis of everything around us. But mankind's understanding of the world is misguided. Mankind seeks rationale through the visible, instead of understanding the Source Of All and how God chooses to speak to each and every one of us. We are not the creators. We are the created. We are children learning to understand His words, but too often we are caught up in the magic of what appears to be reality. And in that, the perspective of our own lens of understanding is reversed, until we are able to recognize this simple truth and learn to see it from the other point of view.

For me, I sought quantifiable results – but with an open mind. Eventually, I began to understand I was seeing everything from a distorted viewpoint – a viewpoint I came to realize was because I was seeing everything in reverse. If a person is to look into the large side of a telescope, nothing would be seen – not even the stars. For me, in realizing I was viewing everything from the wrong end of the telescope, I was eventually able to see the stars – and in that, see light. It was a change that dramatically shifted the tide in the way I sought to understand everything around me. That particular shift in viewpoint was the moment science fell by the wayside, and I began to see the world as God was trying to help me see it. It was a gut punch to my ego, but necessary for my personal journey. Science was the method that God chose to initially communicate with me to help me see. I would go on to learn that God seeks to communicate with everyone in three specific ways. While each of these three ways are still tailored to the ability for each person's level of understanding of His language, the three methods He chooses to deliver his message are consistent for everyone, abridged for understanding.

In the first of the three methods, God communicates through the very world around us – in whatever means possible, through whatever sources of influence can help guide us. This is often the hardest to recognize in the beginning, but observed much more easily once spiritual strength has been achieved. The experience can be a moment as simple as crickets chirping at a certain time or a butterfly landing on your arm as a song is playing certain words that are needed to be heard. It could be a bird slicing through your path on the interstate or a gentle breeze at a specific time. Nature is the vessel for the divine voice of God and all of the guardian angels around us. I like to believe that our guardian angels are constantly offering guideposts to help our recognition of divine influences throughout our journey – though only in hindsight can many be seen with clarity.

The second method God uses to communicate is through the form of another person. This is a gray area many people are taught to notice, but few understand how to interpret. We have all heard of the concept of angels in disguise: the homeless man on the street, the beggar asking for food, etc. However, in modern times it is hard for the mind to rationalize the manifestation of an angel though these means. But rest assured, it happens – though probably in a way that is not well understood. God uses the people around us to guide us. By the use of people as guides, we have to listen to everything in the moment – all variables and nuances occurring in every instance.

Eventually we learn to discern His voice through others, and then we become tasked with learning how to respond. Perhaps a vision led to a spiritual test in the earthly walk. Perhaps a random person says something as simple as, "I hope you know someone is looking out for you" and it is The Lord offering a voice of reassurance in times of hope and strife, unbeknownst to the person offering those words. Perhaps it is a person asking for money who will undoubtedly use the money for harm – but the result would be the necessary point of redirection for that individual to find God. I'm not saying it is important to support bad or even the good decisions people make, but the walk is built upon knowing when you have been called to respond, despite reasoning of the mind. We are all called to respond at times that may seem uncertain in reasoning. But it is important to remember that our words and actions are not our own. Whether through ego or spirit, they are compelled by All That Is to affect the moment in the way it is supposed to happen at that exact time. We are vessels, as is everyone unto us. Every possibility is correct, though every action creates ripples in the great ocean of the journey. Sometimes the ripples counteract oncoming waves. Sometimes the ripples build to a point of a tsunami. This is the power of words and with every action or interaction in life, a new ripple is placed into the spiritual aether.

    The third way God communicates is in direct communion with each of us. This can happen by way of a divine spiritual encounter – perhaps an angel appears before you. Perhaps God's voice rings out in the silence. But, it also happens to everyone every single night in dreams, though it takes practice to be able to hear His words or even recall a dream. Dreams are perhaps the easiest method to begin hearing His voice – mostly because even science offers no rationale to dreams. Our mind has yet to be preconditioned to dismiss them in their entirety, though we rarely question their purpose. Despite some people experiencing bizarre dreams that seem to embody earthly experiences, everything holds meaning. It is only in understanding that dreams are the spiritual playground for the soul which gives way to divine visions and eventually experiences with angels, that the understanding of the spiritual world begins to fall into focus. As is with everything, it takes work and practice to learn the language of God – and knowing that His conversation will occur in whatever way speaks best to you. For me, science got me there, but faith kept me going. It has been a journey so awe-inspiring that I still get excited about every experience and look forward to every time I close my eyes. And – when I do close my eyes, He speaks. When I open my eyes, I find myself walking by faith. Everything else in the world is second to Him, and serves only as a vessel for His voice.

...

The Turn Out Of The Darkness

The first five books of the Bible (or Torah) hold a grand metaphorical meaning that is often overlooked in lieu of the written words. To most, the first five books of the Bible explain the origins of mankind and a potentially literal definition of how mankind came to be. But if I could emphasize anything up unto this point, I would want it to be that our oldest ancestors understood the language of the soul – a divine way of communicating with the spirit. They realized that every word written would stand the test of time and one day permeate the ego and reach the souls of those seeking to understand. With great care, they took every effort to ensure the delivery of the message in every conceivable level of understanding possible through written word alone. So it should be important to understand the first five books of the Bible are five great acts to a divine play of life, loss, and Love. Any screenwriter or playwright will tell you that the most optimal number of acts to tell a story is five. And though the number five holds a special significance spiritually and in divinity, there is an even more special structure to how the first five books were created.

When the names of the books are translated into their root meanings, it becomes evident the first act is "The Beginning" (Genesis). Exodus can best be defined as "Wandering." The third book, Leviticus, should best be understood as "And He Called." The fourth act of the divine play of life is "Into the Desert" – though the literal translation of the fourth book is "Numbers." The archetypal meaning of the original Hebrew word for Numbers (as well as the theme that permeates the book) is the journey into the desert after a specific moment of The Lord's calling. The final act of Deuteronomy should be observed as "Into The Promised Land." This book tells the story of reaching the final destination on a journey that all began with Genesis, followed by the wanderings into Exodus, waiting to hear His Voice as the journey into the desert began, and finally seeing the destination in sight. The meanings to the last three books are the most overlooked and misunderstood because the titles have not transcended into common use throughout the evolution of language. But in understanding the titles in this manner, it then becomes easier to understand how the first five books parallel a journey – a progression of nearly every event and every moment experienced. From the micro to the macro level, the story is told through the five acts required to share the story of life, loss and Love.

Gravity Calling

The year of thirty began my journey in absolute darkness – my Genesis. Six months in, my eyes had adjusted to the darkness. With that one call to Bryan, I began to observe the dim flickering of my pilot light inside and began the turn out of the darkness. Though I didn't know it then, my walk in life would parallel to my spiritual journey. Every action, every job, every interaction with another would in fact hold a spiritual counterpart as I would learn to see in hindsight. But over the journey, hindsight and the present moment found themselves to be bound by a lesser amount of time as my spirit grew in its childhood. And though I held onto science in the beginning, it eventually would be cast aside as I continued onward into spiritual communion with the angels, and eventually with God. While I once thought the journey was about finding the destination, I came to realize as the year of 2013 came to a close, that the journey is the destination – every end point is a new starting line. Through every experience I have had in my earthly walk, there are echoes of spiritual movements forward. Throughout the three years of my spiritual journey, I can only say in hindsight that I had to experience a series of events in my life prior to, and after my Genesis in order for me to see the beauty held within the human experience. I came to know these experiences as life, loss, and Love, and found that Love was the bookend on either side from where the Source originated and found resolve.

To experience life, loss, and Love through the eyes of the human mind (the ego), and to experience through the eyes of the soul would become the mile markers along the journey.

Kindred Souls

The reason behind the experience of our time here on Earth would eventually be revealed as the way we use our time here to experience the best Love story ever told. Though it would take a lifetime to realize the story was already in motion and to truly see God's Love and His plans for me, it would only take a few moments of clarity while standing in the sands of the desert to see how my Not-So-Cinderella story was being written in my earthly walk all along – and in that, the best story I'll ever come to know. And though it took several chapters to set the stage for how my Genesis began and how my eyes started to adjust to the darkness, this is the point where the story really just begins to be told.

Pilot Lights

If I could imagine the way the world must appear to the angels in the heavens, I have to believe that Earth is enveloped in darkness. Every person – whether they believe in God or not – is represented by a dimly lit light, like the light of a candle flickering to the heartbeat of their soul. The light is only bright enough to barely illuminate the radius of their earthly body. Perhaps, this is why humans identify themselves as a body with a soul versus a soul bound by a body. The only thing spiritually visible to a person is the presence of his body. Outside of the radius, the light is obstructed by the densest of fog. When people find the company of others during their wanderings on Earth, they group themselves together – creating a light that is just slightly stronger than theirs alone, granting a greater comfort of existence in the darkness. People begin to navigate using the light of others to illuminate the world around them. In this soft glow, people find comfort and peace – the product of seeing more light than a single body emits alone.

The soft glow of this light and dimly lit flickering of the souls is safety amidst the darkness. Though the eyes may see a world around them, the soul recognizes only light and darkness. And in that recognition, every decision a person thinks he makes is an internal call to the creation of light. There is only one impetus – and that is to see; to illuminate the surroundings. The soft glow of the lights serves as hope for clarity, for understanding. Every decision in life, every encounter, every circumstance that seems bound by earthly rationale is simply the desire to illuminate the surroundings with light. There is no other product. All of the details and nuances that consume the mind in the earthly experience are just musings of others in how light of greater intensity can be created. But they are just that – musings. Musings serve as a mildly interesting way to view the creativity in how others perceive how light can be created. Some musings serve as gentle reminders to the soul – calls home in the darkness. Others serve as distractions from the journey. The musings of highest value are in art – all forms. The motions of a dance, the sounds of song, the colors and expressions in a painting, the palpitations in poem and prose – these are the musings of the soul. With each musing, the soul receives a gentle nudge to the direction of the light within.

Each nudge creates a small recognition of the divine light from whence we were birthed. It doesn't matter in what musing a person finds a call to home – everyone can acknowledge the nudges to a greater call within, though bound by the barriers the mind creates in understanding the physical world as reason. If seen in the metaphor of light, each musing creates a flicker inside – enough to catch the attention of the body wherein the flicker resides, but not enough to fuel the ignition of the flame or guide the person to the light by flicker alone.

Pilot Lights

And often, the quest for what caused the flicker is enough to distract someone from determining what the flicker was in the first place, for most are unaware of their own pilot light inside.

And while it would seem that evil must exist in the darkness based on the concepts of Heaven and Hell and all that we are taught to believe as children, there is no evil – only light. Often questions arise about how such a great and loving God could allow evil to exist or for negative circumstances to happen. The answer is so simple that it is often missed along the way: there is only light. God did not create evil. He is light. We are light. All beings are light, though some have just not figured out this part of the journey. Evil and darkness could best be seen as ego's desire to darken the light of others in preservation of one's own familiarity and comfort of his own soft-lit surroundings. For if another's light has more strength than one's own light within, the greater light will serve as a call of attraction to the company of others – creating a soft glow of hope in a motion away from the presence of the light in whence they once stood. When the landscape of the soft glow of lights bound by the strength of a person's light comes under jeopardy or loss, a person will typically do everything he can to ensure he maintains the company of others in order to hold that certain comfort and peace he has come to know. This is essentially life – the preservation of what we have come to know as our strength.

Acknowledgement that another light exists in greater strength and illumination than one's own is a threat to the safety and protection that has been created among the pilot lights of others. The light of greatest strength and intensity provides a concept of greater safety and illumination and will attract others – like insects attracted to a light in the darkness. And while some people's lights may flare up in strength and intensity in recognition of faith in God, others may dim, but are never completely extinguished. The world is filled with pilot lights all aching for the potential to play their role in helping illuminate the world in light. Darkness is only a great veil to help each person understand his own light within. For how can someone understand his purpose and reason in existence if he does not first understand light? And how can light be understood without first starting in darkness? For what is darkness, but the absence of light?

When the journey begins, the pilot light is dimmed to near-darkness – be it through divine intervention or personal decisions. During this time, it takes the eyes time to adjust. The darkness isn't completely black, though it may seem that way at first. Though there is still a pilot light within softly illuminating the surroundings, the familiarity of the light of others having been removed causes the eyes to readjust their sensitivity to the more dimly lighted surroundings. Once the eyes of the soul adjust and take notice of the beacon – the flickering flame of the pilot light, the journey toward the light begins – and the closer one comes to his light, the brighter it becomes.

With every step forward, spiritual growth occurs, spiritual sensitivity increases, and the veil of darkness in the world begins to be lifted. In these days, the blind will see, the deaf will hear, and the immovable can be moved. In exploration of the

Pilot Lights

light, what gives the light fuel, and how to make the light brighten, one experiences the path to enlightenment that may have once seemed like a spiritual fairytale of sorts. And eventually, in the end, one will begin to understand the flame is one-half of a great circuit fueled by Love, whereby the other half of the circuit can be completed through the union of two souls. When two like flames raging ferociously by the fuel of the spirit come in close proximity with each other and arc, the result is a blinding light that illuminates the heavens. This is the light I would begin to experience in the years to follow finding my pilot light within – a Love like no other I have ever known, though I thought I had once Loved beyond the bounds of any conceivable definition of Love once before. But before I could fully understand Love in the way that God has truly planned for each of us, I would have to first see Love radiating through the experiences of life and loss, all through the lenses of others in order to fully understand the gravity at stake.

Tangled

The recognition of my pilot light was the beginning of the end to my Genesis. As I journeyed forward, I was also beginning to understand the voice of God through the dreams and visions I began to have. While His words were extremely broken in my limited amount of understanding, the importance was that I had taken notice. It was in this notice that the next steps of my journey began. This new starting line would be marked by loss – and the spiritual recognition therein. It was a symbolic ending to the darkness I had been experiencing during my Genesis. It was the first time my soul would take notice of the world around me – an awareness that could only have occurred because of my recognition of the pilot light beginning to illuminate the view. During this first time that I would experience loss spiritually through the eyes of another – and ultimately witness this loss wrapped up in unyielding Love, marked the beginning of my Exodus – the first steps out of the darkness I had found myself in nearly a year prior. It arrived in the fashion of an unsuspecting phone call on Memorial Day weekend in 2012. Up to this point, learning to traverse the darkness and find recognition in my pilot light was all that I had known. But now as it began to illuminate my surroundings, the world through my spiritual eyes began to fall into view.

Over my lifetime, I had suffered the loss of other family members, though the closest loss I had ever experienced was that of Bryan's father, my uncle. Loss always seemed to be something that was unavoidable and could happen at anytime to each and every one of us. Not to sound disheartening, but I was never emotionally swayed by loss. I always found peace in knowing a person's soul was in a better place and that is as far as I allowed my mind to traverse. It was a blind faith I lived by – perhaps to just keep any sad feelings at bay. It was not until I began to experience the spiritual awakening during my journey that my understanding of life and Love would begin to take shape – but it had to begin by me witnessing it through the form of loss. Though I would not necessarily know this moment as the start of my Exodus then, these were the first days of this portion of my journey.

In the beginning days of my Exodus, I had begun to experience angelic encounters in the heavens and brushes with God – though He had yet to reveal Himself in appearance, only through voice. By this point, I had begun to have a completely different outlook on life. Though, with every step forward, I still mistakenly thought I had accomplished the next divine task placed before me – as if everything was linear in the spiritual world, but alas it is not. I was no longer seeing the world as people. Instead, I saw them as souls. It was around this time that I had begun to distance myself from most everyone in my life in order to focus on my personal growth, though it would take a few more months of understanding before I completely realized their absence was required for my walk. I still received invites to all of the nights out with my old friends. However, I found myself rarely taking anyone up on the invites. I showed up to some events, however emotionally distant and unattached from everyone I likely appeared. I was an observer. It was the time in my journey that I didn't speak, but rather listened to and observed everyone around me. I mistakenly thought my presence was a show of support to them, when in truth, I would later learn that presence is only necessary in egoic support. In spiritual support common rules do not apply. But it was a necessary step forward for me to understand the world as seen through my awakening eyes.

So on Memorial Day weekend, after a long day of spending time boating with around twenty people I had once built into my life, one of the guys that I had become friends with received a call that would forever change his life. As the sun was setting on our boat ride home, the call received informed Josh that his brother had passed away. His brother was only 27 years old and left a daughter behind near the age of my daughter at that time. Perhaps it was how his brother's situation was so close to mine that it caused my soul to take notice. His death was completely unexpected, and as I sat there I watched how everyone on the boat reacted. This was the first time I could see the spiritual colors of those very people I had built into my life in the years prior. While no one had ever met his brother, most sat in silence. One person even became angry at Josh when he took his emotions out by punching a pillow below in the cabin. A few teared up after seeing Josh's heartbreak. Another continued to ask him questions he didn't want to answer. All in all, it was safe to say that no one knew what to do. I, too, sat in silence as only an observer. I had not said many words to anyone throughout the afternoon, leaving myself time to focus on my thoughts as I tried to get a tan. But this time, there were no words that could be said in the moment...so I observed.

When I returned home, thoughts were racing through my mind. My soul felt the gravity of Josh's Love for his brother come crashing down in an instant. It was a Love that broke the bounds of any Love for another that I had ever witnessed before, and my soul experienced it snapping in two. But perhaps, it was not any different than what I had experienced before. Perhaps this was just the first time I felt the loss through the eyes of another or with the eyes of my soul gaining vision. From the boat ride back to the marina and all of the way through to this day, my soul experienced a previously unknown hurt for Josh's loss. In the days following, I would witness as no one came to his support during his loss. I witnessed as he experienced his Genesis of sorts – not dissimilar from what I had experienced in my life a year prior – though his darkness came in the form of the loss of a Loved one. In the darkest moment of his life, no one was there for him. He was experiencing the house of egoic friends crumble around him in the wake of his loss as I had just experienced in the wake of my financial collapse. So I offered anything I could for him. I offered to help with the funeral. I offered to help in whatever way he needed. The important thing for him to know was that I was there for him – and not even "I" as in the sense of my earthly identity – it was God using me to let Josh know that He was there for him as well. My soul was an open doorway for Josh to commune with God as needed and I was there in physical presence. It was a bridge between two peoples when he lacked faith in both.

The day after his loss, I wrote about my thoughts initially as an emotional outpouring in search of clarity. It was in this time of my journey that I had begun to find understanding of the spiritual components in my thoughts through the words I would write – and this was one of those times I sought understanding. I found that when I wrote, most of the words exited my mind through my fingertips in unedited form – and only in the hindsight of what was written, could the greatest amount of understanding be gleaned for my journey. Thoughts in abstract bounced around my mind as they gave rise to many of the analogies that would appear in my writings, all in an effort so that I could seek further understanding upon reflection. But after completing my written thoughts about Josh's loss, I decided to pass them onto him in hopes that it would give him hope and faith during his time of sorrow. The words eventually went on to be used as the eulogy for his brother. Unbeknownst to me heading into the funeral, I was the only person asked to speak during the funeral other than Josh, who led the funeral. I honestly couldn't help but tear up as the gravity of the moment hit me while I spoke. In Josh's hardest time, only four people he knew made an appearance at the

Gravity Calling

funeral (including myself and an ex-girlfriend of his). These are the words God helped me deliver to Josh's family that day:

...

    We are all tangled in something greater than the mind can comprehend. And whether we choose to compartmentalize each major moment and the wake of emotions that flood our very being in the aftermath there in, or embrace the ride like a tumbleweed subjected to the desert wind – one thing remains true: Love is our greatest common denominator. That little four letter word that says so much in one short syllable – 2 consonants and 2 vowels – attempts to define an aspect of life that is truly inexplicable....the ineffable existence of our consciousness and how it resonates with its counterpoint in another. That harmony is truly rare. Maybe it is appropriate that the first vowel in that little four-letter word is "o" for it is the only letter with no defined beginning or end. Or maybe it is representative of a point so infinitely small, but so significant, as it is the definition of everything that is and everything that isn't. But, I prefer to think of it as a circle of resonance like a raindrop colliding with another body of water that sends a shockwave of vibrations outward from its very impact. Everything is disrupted and touched in the wake. There is no better explanation as to what Love is, than that.

    And if that is Love, that is also the definition of life – the ripples that resonate through a person, a family, friends, and all those that are connected to someone who has left a resonance on this Earth. This past Memorial Day, I witnessed life – quite possibly for the first time without the blinders or shades that have historically prevented me from truly understanding everything around me. I watched as one of my best friends, and brother to Adam, received a call that no one ever wants to receive. I watched as 20+ of his closest friends all sat in silence on the boat ride back to the marina. I watched as many of them shed tears – no one quite sure how that moment extended to us – but fully aware that we were all impacted in that aroma of time. I didn't personally know Adam – nor did the majority of the people sitting on that boat – but we did know Josh. And to witness how Josh handled those moments and to realize the resonance that Adam imparted during his life – not only sent shockwaves to Adam's closest of kin, but to everyone touched by someone he knew.

For those that didn't know Adam and to be touched by him through a degree or two of separation, must truly represent the force that Adam brought to this Earth. One raindrop, colliding with a body of water so hard that the ripples extend further than just those it initially comes in contact with. I can't begin to comprehend being in the situation that his family – or most importantly his daughter – will forever be forced to endure. And endure is an appropriate word, because someone so Loved and who brought so much life will forever and always remain in the hearts and minds of those he touched. The seemingly insurmountable challenge of taking the next baby step forward, having the next holiday without, attempting to somehow see beyond the void, the crater left in his absence – will define each and every person that ever knew Adam from this very point forward – especially his daughter Lydia.

It is those baby steps that we need to help Adam's family begin to take. It is the very purpose we share and the common bond among each and every one of us. Lydia has every amazing year ahead of her and should forever remember her daddy in the same vein that has brought us all together in this moment – to remember Adam as a blessing this Earth was privileged to have hosted during his 27 years. Please help us ensure Lydia will forever sustain that memory, and one day, be able to understand the outpouring of support from everyone that was ever touched by Adam's life.

Gravity Calling

For it is in these special moments that Love and life are celebrated until we all meet again in the presence of the Great Divine.

...

The words spoke as much to my soul as my soul was speaking the words to others. This was the first time I would visualize people, actions, and most importantly Love, in terms of resonance and ripples. It did not strike me until the moments after reading what I had written that the very essence of life and loss is Love. It is a warmth that ties life together. I had allowed my writing to be a freeform way to express my thoughts in the aftermath of his news the day prior, and in those thoughts, I found clarity in my spiritual understanding of the moment. Though I would not fully understand the gravity of timeless spiritual Love for another year or two, the clarity offered to me in the words I had written served as a guidepost and guiding light to Love as the beginning and the end and our reason in life. The words I had written caused me to begin to seek understanding of how my spirit recognized why, in someone's time of loss, Love served as the strength. I once believed that Hope was the strength of the soul, found in times of strife and in times of loss. But spiritually, I now recognized it was Love. It was always Love – and somehow, I had missed the signs.

Midnight Red

Why is the gravity of Love so difficult to put into words? Hallmark's very existence would lead us to believe that the volume of Valentine's cards, Love You cards, Miss You cards, and Thinking of You cards that exist still can't express the unique kind of Love we find in another. For mankind, we have evolved to communicate through the five senses used to understand the world around us. Concepts and ideas can be communicated through the simple action of touch, an aroma, a palette of flavors, an action, or even just by looking into another's eyes – but most importantly through words and sound. Though speech and writing would be the methods that most people would identify as the primary ways to express thoughts – concepts can be communicated just as easily through music, tones and subtle vibrations. But, words alone lack clarity.

Though words are mankind's best effort at a single means of physical communication, it is the combination of words with the other senses that can evoke an even greater level of communication. Think of how a song can say so much more to someone than just the words alone or how a movie can add so much more depth than could otherwise be presented through the dialogue, the story, the visuals, or the soundtrack alone. To add another layer of depth, think of how much more of an

Gravity Calling

impact the experience of a song or movie can be when experienced in the company of a significant other – holding them, kissing them, a subtle touching of hands brushing at a special moment in a movie, a moment of dancing and staring into another's eyes during a romantic song, the fusing of aromas in the atmosphere at that particular time. These are the moments that overpower the human mind and invoke levels of depth within each and every one of us that cannot be explained through traditional means. These moments are seemingly a convergence of great odds, yet are comprised of well-articulated, complex thoughts architected of divine construction.

Even beneath these layers that comprise the most overpowering of feelings, exists one more layer of language occurring at such a depth that most people can only describe as a gut feeling – though it is so much more. It is the moment an inner voice calls out and offers reassurance for the choice in a decision, offers an instant understanding of a person's character just from acknowledgment of their physical presence, or the voice of surrender to the soul's recognition in its counterpoint in another – the moment a person "just knows." It is the romance of the soul – words penned in every shade of midnight-red, written upon a canvas of the whitest of light. This is the divine language of Love – a concept that words and metaphors will always fall short in conveying.

Though there are more than 200,000 words that comprise the English language, there are not enough words or combinations of words to adequately describe the context of life, loss, and Love. Only through the artful use of words, analogies, symbols, pacing, flow, rise and fall of the phrasing of each sentence can a call to the soul be evoked. And in the midst of the artful use of words, that which is not directly said amongst the words holds within it a greater gravity than that which is put into words. It is the space between two notes that holds the grace in song; the words left unsaid among that which is said that is the language of the soul. Words serve only as a forceful attempt at knocking, while the artful structure of words and verse can serve as a vehicle to deliver the unsaid – and in that, the soul can find truth. But what if a person were able to communicate directly in romance to the soul? And why does it take a palette of two hundred thousand words, specific settings, scenarios, sounds, and lighting to know that the art created will only speak in indirect conversation?

The answer does not lie in the attempt at conveying concepts, but rather the barrier of understanding. Since the beginning of time, man has chosen how to understand communication instead of allowing communication to dictate how he/she should understand the message. This is distinctly different than "understanding purpose/intent" or "seeing the underlying message" beneath the literal interpretation. The words may read the same; the meaning may sound the same; but in practice, these concepts are entirely different. The ability to allow communication to dictate understanding is found in the complete surrender of senses to the message, thus allowing the senses to collect, understand, and interpret everything in the moment – every nuance, every unspoken detail. There is no mental choice in what one thinks the message conveys, only knowledge of what the words mean to the inner self. Only through the removal of all preconceived notions regarding everything a person chooses to think they know of the world (egoic interpretation) and viewing the world through the eyes of a child is it possible to begin to discern this level of communication. Everything – all of creation – is founded on this very premise wherein the unraveling of the greatest layers of depth in communication occur.

    The side of logic tends to battle through dialogue by using the word "I" in interpretation – "I think," "I know," etc. This side – which is better known as ego – will inevitably suppress understanding by becoming lost in the argument with itself during the dialogue, thus distracting the mind from the true message the counter-side first acknowledged. The side of the ego is also the culprit to the manifestation of fear – which by definition, is the mind's recognition of an inevitable fight/surrender to a concept that it is not fully capable of comprehending in the context of the moment. Some people are able to suppress fear by simply choosing not to understand – mostly because it is simply easier than any attempt at understanding. Others may learn to suppress fear by way of complete surrender to the acceptance of the unknown – popularly known as faith. But, most will stand conflicted – unsure of the message, constantly searching to understand the ongoing inner dialogue, perhaps even claiming "faith" without fully succumbing to its very definition.

Midnight Red

    Depending on the message, some will play the proverbial role of the actor for a script they believe defines how they should react – often becoming lost in the muscle-memory-like actions they believe best demonstrate what others expect as a response. Some will blissfully miss the whole picture because they are consumed in the magic of each moment. Regardless of each person's mindset, feeling the unmistakable gravity carried through words (both spoken and unspoken) evokes a call to our origin and thusly the hand that penned our existence. Through the artful use of words we learn to communicate through the language of the soul – the language of life, loss, and ultimately Love. And hopefully, through words, the gravity of all that we attempt to communicate will reach the destination wrapped up in the intended ribbons and labels, able to be opened for the abundance of spiritual Love housed within the packaging. For life is a Love story bound through the graces of God's hand – words intending to express His Love for all and how it is to be experienced on Earth, aching for the soul to hear, to see. For so in the Word, is everything – and in everything, so Is; and All That Will Be is wrapped up in a blanket of His divine penmanship, artfully crafted in everything that exudes Love so that one day we may each understand the language penned by His hand.

Seventy-Seven

Eighteen months from the start of my Genesis marked the beginning of my Leviticus – the moment when I could say with absolution that God had spoken to me directly, not just in a way I could understand, but a way that Bryan could and hopefully others would as well. This was the moment "He Called" and marked the end of my days of wandering in Exodus from the darkness. The moment of hearing His Voice was the greatest moment of my journey unto this point. On an evening in January, Bryan and I had increased our conversations to multiple times a week with each call generally lasting a couple of hours. Our original intention of understanding dreams had fully transitioned to understanding how God was working in our lives and communicating with us through visions and the world around us. By this point, we had each experienced multiple angelic encounters and had each heard the voice of God. However, we were still searching to understand the chasm between the spiritual and earthly worlds – how to bridge the two worlds as one.

Over the previous months we had begun to realize that our conversations on the phone were as significant as prayer. We came to understand that when souls were driving conversation, God was listening and would respond in ways we would be able to understand. There were numerous phone calls when we would discuss a particular topic and then a seemingly improbable answer would manifest in our earthly walks over the course of the following days. Though it took the discernible eye of the spirit, we noticed and made sure to discuss the occurrences. It was still somewhat hard for us to fully accept by faith alone (without a smidgen of doubt entering the equation) that these occurrences were not our own interpretations used to support our spiritual desires. But, we ventured on. And perhaps the fact we always humbly raised questions instead of formed answers to what we thought we observed was the impetus behind Gods grand intervention to come.

Throughout Bryan's and my random banter during our conversations, we began to call these perceived call-and-response moments between God and our conversations "seven-and-seven moments," which represented a spiritual high-five of sorts. These seven and seven moments could come in the form of a vision one of us had and an experience the other had that supported the other. They could come as shared visions, or even as a moment where God imparted something in a vision that would foreshadow the rise of an earthly equivalent in the following days. It could come from a prayer request and a perceived answer. We took comfort that God was throwing out "atta-boys" to help each of us build confidence in our walks. The use of the term "seven-and-seven moment" at this point in our conversation was so common-place and frequent, we even joked about it becoming mildly off-putting in the midst of conversation.

Seventy-Seven

So on that particular evening in January, Bryan and I were talking about money and windfalls. For me, it was the first time I had discussed my thoughts on money after my financial collapse. I had come to learn that everything that enters into our lives is done so by God's hand. We only have one purpose, and that is to serve Him in the manner He has chosen for us. Along the journey, He provides us the resources we need to find peace and continue onward. As long as we understand and observe that everything is given to us from Him as a vehicle purposed for His divine intention and not earned by our egoic desires, it becomes easier to see there is no need for any material items in our lives. As I discussed these thoughts with Bryan, I made a specific reference to winning the lottery or finding a random sack of money sitting on your doorstep. For most, they would take the money and squander it, or perhaps invest it. Some may even use it for good, but still take a portion for themselves But in this conversation, I made it clear that if something like this were ever to be placed randomly into my life with no apparent spiritual impetus, I could not take one single dollar from the amount to benefit myself. I would not pay off any of the debt that still hung over my head, for it was debt I had accrued while my ego was driving and it was upon me to make good on the financial damage I had allowed my ego to create. Instead, I would deliver the full amount of money in whatever manner God directed me to do.

Our conversation ended on a very high spiritual note. We said our goodbyes and I went to bed. The next morning I awoke feeling extremely refreshed. The morning had an air of certainty, resolve and peace. It was a rare morning that I got ready early before work and was able to relax to some music and meditate before leaving my place. But when the time came to leave, I could never have been prepared for what was to come. As I opened my door to the open-air breezeway that separated the other seven units or so in my building, I looked down before me and saw a bundle of cash sitting on my doorstep. Clearly it was possible that it fell out of someone's pocket, but the bundle was wadded up into nearly the size of a softball. I looked down either side of my hallway. I walked to the stairwell and elevator. I looked in the parking lot. It was clear that no one was recently around that would have dropped it. I picked it up and began to think about the conversation I had with Bryan the previous evening. I stood there in disbelief that a message from God would be so overt in response to the conversation. To this point, any seven and seven moments that Bryan and I had experienced could be left unto interpretation. But this was just the start. (To dispel any doubt for the reader, it is important to understand that Bryan lives four hours away. We also took these types of events very seriously as well – never joking about the gravity they held).

 I walked down to my Jeep, careful to make sure if I saw someone leaving to ask them if they had lost any money. No one was around. When I reached my Jeep, I sat down and unwadded the bills to count the amount I held in my hand. It became apparent there were a lot of smaller denominations that made the bundle appear larger in size, but as I arrived at the final total my jaw hit the ground. I was holding seventy-

Seventy-Seven

seven dollars. I immediately sent Bryan a picture with no context behind the image. He initially thought I was joking with him and called me back immediately to understand what I had found. If there was ever a moment that God disambiguated all of the moments we thought had potentially occurred in our pasts, this was the moment.

But this was just the start of a spiritual test. In truth, $77 is a small amount of money for most people, easily lost in the shuffle of the busy world. But, with this $77, I was now tasked with walking the walk from the conversation the night prior. I was in no rush to make a decision. Instead, I chose to hold onto the cash until I could identify God leading me in a direction. As divine circumstances would have it (and I would only recognize the timing in retrospect days later), on the evening of the seventh day from the original conversation with Bryan, I would see a friend's post (her name is Leah) on a social network. Leah's message was asking for people to help contribute any way they could to help a family she knew rebuild their life after having their house completely destroyed by fire. The following morning – the seventh day from when I found the bundle of money – I would write a divinely inspired letter and deliver it in an unmarked envelope along with the $77 to Leah, so that she could deliver it to her friend. The timing of it all was again, another seven and seven moment that I would only see in hindsight of my actions. And while $77 may not seem like much to help someone who has just lost everything, the last paragraph of the letter hopefully sums up the impetus behind the letter and God's intention in my action.

Gravity Calling

This experience and letter marked the beginning of my Leviticus and my second understanding of the divine language of life, loss, and Love. The letter is included below:

...

    Some say strange things "just happen" but I'm a firm believer in everything having a purpose. Even the seemingly most insignificant things have the potential to play a much more important role in the master plan. Nothing could exemplify this better for me than what occurred the morning of January 18th. But to understand the 18th, let's first rewind to the evening of the 17th.

    On the evening of the 17th I was having a philosophical, theological and spiritual discussion with a close friend. During that conversation, we spoke in depth about how our Creator is always guiding us – granting us the decision to acknowledge and follow His leads through life. His "leads" may not come in the forms of answers or guidance we expect to see and therefore most do not understand how to truly experience the walk within their own faith. Most people expect when they ask for _____ , the only answer is to receive exactly what they asked for. To most, anything less cannot be divine or the product of His doing. The misnomer is in the most obvious flaw – that flaw is that we have no right to ask for anything. We have already been given everything. And within that space, we serve as vessels for our Creator – to follow the leads He has set forth and be able to positively share His intention within that space.

    I could go off into a tangent about how egos and earthly perceptions cloud our understanding of the marvelous leads that are constantly set forth before us, but I'll save that discussion for a later time. The important part I want to communicate is the main topic of the conversation from the evening of the 17th – which is also why I am writing you this letter.

Seventy-Seven

During that conversation, my friend and I spoke at great lengths about the people who ask God for money or wealth, and believe their prayers go unanswered (pretty much, this was the focal point of the conversation). Truthfully, most people believe that only they can manufacture their own wealth and God won't answer the "please let me win the lottery" prayer. But the main point of our discussion was that most people won't acknowledge when God bestows an opportunity to do great things with what he has given – regardless of our perception of the significance, because definitions of significance vary from person to person. A boat to one person is a yacht to another – or that very boat could mean an opportunity to feed a family. Perception is all in the eye of the beholder. Within the context of our conversation, we discussed how "windfalls" of income shouldn't have a defined set of zeros attached to it. Nor should a "windfall" have to be delivered in expected mechanisms such as winning the lottery, receiving an inheritance, or (and this next part is important) finding a sack of money at your front door.

The conversation could not have had a greater stamp of His approval than what occurred the morning of the 18th. As I rushed out the door to go to work, I opened the door and there in front of me, in the midst of the highly trafficked hallway of my condo complex, was a wadded up bundle of cash. I looked around thinking it was a joke at first. But as I realized no one was (or had been) recently around and this money was clearly in front of me & intended for my eyes, that this was God's acknowledgement of my prior night's conversation. Within this moment was the opportunity for me to demonstrate that I could mean the words I had spoken the previous night.

While the amount of cash may not seem significant, therein lies a greater acknowledgement. The amount was $77. For anyone familiar with *the numeric significance within the evolution of humanity, that person would easily be able to acknowledge the number 7 has always carried a divine significance. It is a spiritual number of sorts. Now I could again digress on topics of the history of linguistics and how language evolved around the world and how numbers were initially formed, but that could be a book in and of itself. For now, please trust in me when I say that the number 77 carries a far greater significance in our earthly and spiritual journey than most people will ever realize. Basically, this was God communicating with me on terms that I could clearly and unmistakably understand. For someone else, it may have been another method. For me, in this moment, I heard everything He was saying.*

I acknowledged that this $77 represented a far greater purpose than I could understand. Several days passed with no signs of what to do. I wasn't actively looking, nor was I anxious to make an irrational decision. I knew that somehow passively, I would be able to be a vessel for His intention. So it came as no surprise that a very dear friend, Leah, posted on Facebook a brief story about your situation and how we could all help. I knew in that very moment that I had the full acknowledgement of God's intention with the small "windfall" outside of my door.

Perhaps the $77 may not mean anything to you directly. Perhaps it will be able to be used with the medical costs. Perhaps the intention was not in the $77 itself, but to acknowledge that God somehow foresaw the events occurring in your family's life and also foresaw the amount of Love that would be spilled forth among friends, family and even those just touched by your situation. Perhaps, the $77 is just God saying "I'm here" and maybe that is the most important point of all of this. I can't be entirely certain of his intention of this $77 for you, but I hope that somehow with-

Seventy-Seven

in the money, the story, or somewhere in between, that you can find peace, trust and faith in Our Creator.

- Warmest Blessings -

...

Unconditionally, Ferociously

Nearly two years into my journey, the portion of the race that paralleled Leviticus was nearing its end – a starting line originally marked by the divine seven and seven moment of the $77 that occurred a few months prior. But before I could embark into the desert to experience the next starting point of my journey, God intended for me to witness one last great act of Love, which too was wrapped up in life and loss. The prior six months had involved a roller coaster of personal experiences that had all tugged at my heartstrings, attempting to prime my heart to Love again. But it would take witnessing this one act of true Love through the eyes of another to help me understand everything that I had been missing in my previous marriage.

If I was ever asked where the greatest hole in my heart resided, I could always point to the place that held the act of being Loved unconditionally, ferociously, in an on-fire-kind-of-Love way. I never felt that I had a problem loving in that way – and at one time I thought I was Loved in return. But in moments of having a Father's Day forgotten in a young marriage, not being able to recount one simple gesture of affection or even an acknowledgement of Love beyond the words, my heart became numb to that particular locale in my heart. And while I would overlook it during my marriage in part because I would rather Love unconditionally with no reciprocal Love than to not Love at all, I couldn't help but always feel there was a longing for that one simple fulfillment. Maybe that is why in the years following my divorce it was so important for me to help others be happy – because I desperately longed to feel that in return from others.

Over the years following my divorce, I watched as my best friend's marriage came to an end. I watched as my relatives struggled through their marriages. Bryan's marriage of 17 years came to an end as well. And though there were glimmers of Love radiating from some people I knew, overall I couldn't help but feel like the idea of being Loved in the way I wanted to Love another was nothing more than a helpless romantic falsehood that I would somehow never experience. I prayed a lot over that particular area of my life, and I tried to find comfort that God would not leave that particular prayer unheard. But as my journey was still developing in spiritual strength, my ability to trust completely was not yet in motion. Sometimes I think I must be the neediest child known to God – someone whom He, Himself has spoken to directly so that I may find resolve and peace, allowed angels to appear with answers, and even provided communication through the very world around me. I can't help but think that sometimes He face-palms Himself over the naiveté of my ways and has a slight chuckle. But it is all part of the process, which is why the Leviticus aspect to the journey became so important.

In all of my life I can only recount one moment of unconditional, ferocious Love that happened to me – and that was with my very first girlfriend in college; a relationship that only lasted six months. That particular memory could have been puppy Love, but it was the outpouring of spirit that my girlfriend-at-the-time put into celebrating our first Valentines Day together. She took the time to surprise me by hiding little things in my car and in places that I would find throughout the day. She didn't know it, but I inadvertently saw her begin to hide things in my car while I was at work, so I continued to watch. I watched her movements, the care, the way she was trying to sneak around quietly without letting me, or even the world know what she was doing. All along I just watched and smiled. It wasn't in the items themselves or even in the way she chose to surprise me throughout the day, but rather it was the way she moved, the way she thought, the way her soul was captured in every effort she made that spoke to mine. None of my other friends saw it, or even understood it. But to me, it is the only memory I have of that kind of outpouring from one soul to another.

It was the only time I would witness a Love like that until this new point in my journey – a time wherein I would have to see it through the eyes of my best friend and the new girl he was dating. And though the moment I want to share is the moment I saw Love appear again in an unconditional, ferocious kind of way, I also had to watch as their relationship came to an end not too long after. It was in the complete observance of not just that moment of life and Love emanating from both spirits, but the loss suffered through the relationship coming to an end that served as the entire picture in understanding my third lesson in the divine language of life, loss, and Love.

It was a complicated situation with a failing long-distance marriage on one side. It took everything I could do to remove the pre-conceived notions I had about relationships in order to witness the extraordinary that happened that day. And I have to believe that is what God intended for me to see because I was able to see the movements of two souls entrenched in the most beautiful song, defying the bounds of contrived thinking – though eventually having to find an end because their very foundation was lacking the spiritual foundation to shore everything in place. It would take a lot of thought, introspection, and prayer to fully understand everything I witnessed that day. It was the first time my soul was given hope that a Love like that could exist – if even for just a fraction of a second during the course of a lifetime. It was also the first time God allowed my eyes to be removed from the laws of time in order to see how every action and every word we create serves as a constant rippling effect – a method of redirection from one point to the next.

Into The Aether

Time. We are all defined by a constant state of motion – one fractional moment in time colliding with the next; a series of snapshots chained together with the next creating a movie of static images all held together by one constant: change. To understand that every event, every person, every interaction, every nuance of a moment – all set off a series of unstoppable events until the next interaction redirects the motion to its next destination. It is the basic principle behind creation, and the true definition of eternity. And it is in that definition that life finds its niche. Life may have its beginnings, its endings, its births, its deaths, its Love, its loss. But, to understand that each of these moments is just but a point of redirection for everything connected to its source, is to understand the greater commonality within everyone – we are all just a pigment of a picture, each creating the hues of a greater story being told.

And if it is possible for time to stand still – if for just a moment – and to somehow take that snapshot and see both beyond and within the immediate picture – the pigments of color that are all mixing with each other become apparent; the hues being created; the foundations being layered on top of each other; to understand that this moment is not just the image that is seen, but a snapshot of everything in motion before and after, should bring clarity to the moments that often seem the most cloudy. It is a difficult task at hand, but an invaluable ability once it is learned. For it is within that ability that the challenges of life become easier to deal with and the incomprehensible somehow becomes more relevant than it previously was. It is a moment that art and Love fall into view.

For me, the realization of the afore-mentioned ability – the shining moment where I first saw the big picture – did not occur until I witnessed a series of events unfold one particular night involving a close friend. In retrospect, I wish I had been more attuned to understanding the bigger picture much earlier in my life. I've always been very aware of the interaction of events and how each event has played a role in shaping the bigger picture. The difference in my understanding during this portion of my journey versus my understanding prior, though, is as significant as the first time a person with poor vision puts on a pair of glasses. That person may have been able to see – maybe even to the point they were not quite aware of the details they were missing. But in one moment of clarity when the lenses on the glass alter the light entering the cornea in just a way so as to focus every particle of light into one precise point where every detail, every nuance becomes visible from the hazy mashup of color before – it is in such a comparative moment for me that awareness of the aether became distinctly visible; the aether in which the resonance in one's consciousness became more than just a concept; the inaudible melodies of our beings falling into harmony with one another all cognitively understood and visually represented in my mind. I was seeing something that by all definitions of science was distinctly not there, but something that I was acutely aware of – and in that moment, was visually represented in my mind.

The night began with a dinner at one of the newest and most popular restaurants in town. People filled the room for a friend's 30th birthday bash. My intrigue mounted in anticipation of meeting the new woman in his life – for he had gotten divorced shortly after me, and I was looking for something to hold onto as a beacon of hope that my search would one day begin again. Earlier in the night I had already heard that she was preparing something special for him, so it was understandable that I was intrigued over the way the night would play out. She was steadfast in her approach as being "just friends" and had maintained that veil of secrecy flawlessly to her closest friends over the preceding weeks. The night could have unfolded in any number of ways, and I had to be meticulous in discretely maintaining any fallout, for I was only one of two other people who knew of their secret relationship.

So, when the moment finally arrived when she would grace his birthday bash with her presence, I was unprepared for everything that I would witness. She entered the room fashionably late, courting her only girlfriend – the only other person aware of their relationship. They were wearing matching dresses. Both of them looked stunning – beyond gorgeous – wearing matching sheer black tops with electrifying pink skirts. It was a blend of classy and celebration wrapped up in a sophisticated ensemble. They were both expecting to be noticed with no expectations of subtlety.

Gravity Calling

From the moment they walked in wearing their coordinated dresses, my soul recognized the presence of something special, something rare. It was in that moment time paused for me. That snapshot in time – a blurring of hues in motion all blending together to paint the picture of a promising story yet to be told – all became immediately evident to my eyes and my mind. As just the observer, I captured every detail, every nuance in those initial moments and would continue do so until the night came to an end. I have never felt so emotionally sober where everything I witnessed was affecting me in different ways. It wasn't just the dress or the way her smile fell across her face in a way that would make any guy's heart race. It wasn't just the aura of positive energy emanating from her being. In truth, there was only one small detail that stood out in such a way that would go on to define my perception of her – and it seems on the surface level, so simple. But maybe the complexity of a situation is best illustrated in the simplicity of such a detail. For often, that overlooked detail – so minutely small – is actually the definition of everything that is.

That detail – easily missed by the average onlooker – was a pair of matching necklaces, handmade and coordinated to match their dresses. The necklaces were beaded in a mardi-gras-esque style, with handmade letters spelling out my friend's last name. It became very obvious at this point that her profession as a fashion designer was fully in play in preparation for his birthday. The letters of his last name were hand cut, painted, glued and styled in a way that only someone so emotionally invested could have done. In just a fraction of a moment in time – a nanosecond at best – I observed a detail that would immediately trigger a distinctly different way I would ever view life and human interaction. That trigger brought my soul to life in awareness of their two soul's finding beautiful song with one another – something I had yet to observe since my Genesis. For true song in another is a rare moment indeed. That trigger would go on to open a doorway that evening in visualizing the unseen – the emotional magnitude of order at play in every given situation.

That one little detail sparked my soul with hope and told me everything I needed to know about her. Dismiss the complexities of life. Dismiss preconceived notions as to the proper way events are "supposed" to occur. It was in this moment that I realized there are kinks in the fabric of time, and with each interaction in life, a redirection of our future is made. I could close my eyes and, for the first time ever in my life, visualize everything occurring in the room that evening. I felt the resonance of each person in the room – something of which I was already acutely aware existed. But this time it was different. I visually saw the resonance in my mind – the ripples and complex patterns of platonic solids forming and dissipating in each person's resonance; every pattern interacting with the next – like raindrops hitting a body of water – all creating a certain vibrational pattern in the aether throughout the room; every movement and every action of every person directly causing the vibrational interactions to increase and decrease with proximity to each person's wake.

Gravity Calling

But in those moments, my mind did not stop in awe and wonder of this new visualization. Instead, my mind continued to formulate more in depth visualizations. I saw connected lines – threads in a woven fabric – each tying one person to the next. Those threads intertwined and remained in a constant state of motion. I wouldn't describe the threads as a tangible entity in this visualization, but more of a thread of light. Each thread connected the individual to an event, a place, another person. And similar to the way that two complementary tones create a harmony, or two clashing tones create a dissonance, it was apparent that people, actions and most importantly intentions could cause harmony and dissonance in another and simultaneously cause those beads of light to redirect to other future events, places, people, and times. I was visualizing threads that were by all disparate attempts at a definition, the very fabric of life and the foreshadowing of future affects caused in each nanosecond of that particular snapshot in time.

In light of as many words as it just took to describe this new perception and visualization that my mind was formulating throughout the night, it is important to understand that this visualization was occurring as fast as the neurons in my brain could fire. It was a visualization that was occurring so quickly, I could only define it as my mind was on autopilot in processing this enormous amount of data flowing in. It was all happening subconsciously, but I was consciously aware of my brain at work. There are no words that can truly describe the concept I am attempting to describe – much in the same vein

Into The Aether

as scientists attempting to define a thought or a dream – neither have an effable description. But, the visual representation is important to understand if only for this example of the picture I am painting.

Other details from the night fueled by their song would further add to the collage of images forever captured in my mind. Maybe it was the chalice she professionally decorated with beads, paint, and glitter-glue that spelled out his last name and other cutesy phrases around the bell – a chalice he would take all of his drinks from throughout the evening. Maybe it was the funfetti cake – homemade and carefully decorated by her. Maybe it was the other countless moments of selflessness that she demonstrated in helping his 30th birthday become the best birthday he had ever experienced. Whatever the case, I was not witnessing the actions of someone whose heart wasn't fully invested. In fact, in her every action she spilled forth an abundance of Love – the kind of Love for another that sparked hope within me. I wasn't sure of the reason behind her personal situation or her backstory, but I felt guilty for having preconceived notions and not removing the shackles of conformity from my outlook on her before we met. This was the first time I could see clearly, and I fully attest this clarity to seeing someone I was so in tune with, finding complete harmony in another.

The details that I would observe throughout the night created a visual masterpiece in my mind. The very fabric in the aether, woven from the resonance that our bodies and actions project would leave a visual impression of her that I could not dismiss. My friend saw it in her, and while he probably had no idea of the visual masterpiece at work in my mind, he followed his instincts. For most, instincts are the only queues we have that are unquestionably present, predictably accurate, but have no scientific justification to support their existence. I had never experienced in any relationship, anything similar to the demonstration I witnessed this woman showcase for my friend. There was clearly something I had been missing in every prior relationship that was blatantly obvious in those moments. Later discussions with my friend would further confirm that he too had never experienced such a grand gesture of emotional outpouring in any of his prior relationships. The meticulous care in the details may not seem that big of a deal at first blush, but it was the amount of preparation, the care of perfection that demonstrated everything I needed to know about her.

In the following weeks I would get to know her on a more personal level and come to understand more of the backstory. I watched as their puppy-Love progressed to a full-fledged relationship and eventually roar to an abrupt ending in light of her moving away. I saw the harmony. I saw the potential branches of outcomes – fairytale, tragedy and everything in between – that were constantly being redirected with each moment they spent together and in the time they spent time apart. Every snapshot of those moments – each tied to the next – all held together by the constant, change. Over the growth in my spiritual journey and through communion with God, I came to realize the only thing they were missing was the spiritual foundation in each of their lives that would help them discern their soul's true song. Had that been there, it would have been as magnificent as witnessing two shooting stars collide in the night sky creating a light so bright all of the other stars would fade from view, leaving no chance of their newfound union ever falling away from the other. It would have been the kind of story told through the ages and dreamed upon as children fall asleep in their beds. But for that point in their lives, it was redirection that was necessary for each to learn individually the steps required to experience a Love like that again. For me, witnessing their beautiful song that evening was the spark that allowed hope back into my soul. To find a Love like that was now no longer a question of possibility, but a question of God's intention in my life – one that I would have to wait just a little bit longer to hear His response.

Sand

My journey into the desert – the starting line to my book of Numbers – occurred long before I was aware I had even stepped foot in that direction. I was running blissfully into the sunrise, enjoying my spiritual journey before I ever came to realize I wasn't holding anyone's hand. It would take me actually staring at the Promised Land to realize where I was standing, to realize where I had journeyed from, and to think back over what had just occurred. It was a moment similar to when a child first learns to ride a bicycle. In the beginning the child is afraid of falling over, but he finds strength in training wheels. These wheels serve more as a confidence builder than anything else to the child. Soon after, a child's parent will take the wheels off and run along side of the bicycle holding the back of the seat. Just the very presence of the parent is the confidence needed for the child to learn to ride. As the child picks up speed, the parent slowly pulls away knowing their hand ultimately isn't doing anything anyway, and allows the child to ride off into the distance. Eventually the child crashes or comes to a stop when he realizes he is doing it on his own. But it is the moment when the child turns around and smiles, radiating the abundance of happiness and excitement from his accomplishment, that the parent knows the child is going to be okay. In that very same moment, the child realizes he has found a new starting line, no longer bound by his parents' constant assistance – now just needing occasional guidance along the way. It is not the end of being helped, but the recognition of no longer needing to be carried. This was the place I found myself standing as I gazed at the Promised Land.

I can't help but think how divinely inspired the first five acts of our spiritual journeys are conceived, written and designed. Entry into the desert is marked by times of spiritual trials, demonstrations of the spiritual walk, demonstrations of unending faith in Our Creator. The desert is a place of fasting, a place where a person removes all of the bindings to an earthly life and offers his life to The Almighty. It is a place where death is much more than a possibility – it is a certainty when not properly prepared for. Nearly every religion has mirrored this part of the journey through the exercise of fasting or sabbaticals. Every prophet written about in historic texts once served a portion of their journey in some form of a personal walk with God syphoned from the constraints of earthly influences, being tested in the desert. In nearly every occurrence, there is one commonality – sand. And, I can't think of a more appropriate substance to serve as the foundation for this portion of the journey.

Beneath all of the grains of sand is evidence of times past. If a person is to dig deeply enough, the sands of the desert will reveal civilizations past, ancient structures of unfathomable architecture, and evidence that this generation of mankind is not the first, nor will it be the last that has been allowed to

Sand

grace the Earth with its presence. Beneath the sand in the oceans is evidence of sunken adventures, sunken treasures, and civilizations submerged first by water, then by time. The beaches are the edges of the Earth that separate the land from the great oceans around us – the fringe between the unsteady and sublime. Children find adventures and happiness when playing in sand. And even when beaches are not in close proximity to a child, parents often build sandboxes for their children to play in. Sand is used in the construction of nearly every material known to man – materials that are used to build the most solid structures of the grandest buildings. It is the primary ingredient in concrete as well as the substance used to soften and smooth rough edges of lumber. Sand is used to polish gemstones turning just a rock of the earth into something of intrinsic value, with luster and brilliance. Sand is also the primary substance used in weights – and more importantly, in counterweights for objects needing to balance the force of gravity.

But through it all, sand has one more mesmerizing and complex property that is often overlooked – a property revealed through the application of heat. Only through the application of intense amount of heat, and the gentle breath of cool air against the sand's molten surface is glass created. And how appropriate is it that the very substance used as the foundation for this metaphorical part of the journey is also the very substance that forms the stained glass pieces of our lives? One could even go so far as to say that the breath of life given to our souls is tantamount to our lives being forged from sand into glass. It is only within the broken, rebuilt creations of mankind that the uniqueness of each creation, the Love each of us has to give, the Love we are destined to one day receive, and the true beauty of each of our souls is eventually revealed.

And so, as I found myself staring at the Promised Land, I realized my soul was naked before God – my feet slightly submerged in the very foundation beneath me. I realized I had journeyed a great distance, even if at times I had found myself struggling for traction on my journey into the sun. It was only when the Promised Land fell into view that I understood I was no longer holding the hands of my spiritual elders, guides, or even the hand of God for strength. At some point I had let go, blissfully running into the sun. I now knew the angels and God were always there around me and within; I was no longer bound by hands to hold on. This was the time that my soul would learn to be – now growing up as a child of God. In hindsight, I would realize that the journey into the desert could only have begun when I was able to find hope in Love again – though I would not know it quite on those terms yet.

After the bookend experience of witnessing unconditional Love in my life's version of Leviticus, the series of steps I took into the desert led me further on a path of learning and growth. I would come to realize the first leg of the journey was to learn to see the world through the eyes of a child – my daughter's eyes. The second leg of the journey would involve me learning to more acutely hear His Voice through nature and my surroundings. The third leg of the journey would involve me seeking my spiritual identity – one of the hardest

Sand

steps I struggled to make. But it was during the last steps I took as I stopped to take notice of the Promised Land falling into view, that I realized not only had I been running without holding hands, but the final portion of this journey involved me completing a form of a sabbatical in the midst of modern times – an accomplishment that I can't help but look back and smile at the divine architecture of His plan. And how appropriate would it be that the first steps I would take into the desert sand would be through the eyes of a child? For children find the most blissful joy while playing in the sand.

Playing With Magic

Children hold within their eyes the innocence of vision untainted by ego or by earthly wisdom acquired over a lifetime. Their eyes are full of wonder observing everything around them. Their minds are like sponges soaking up every nuance, every intricacy, every tiny detail that adults often miss in haste. A child's mind assembles all of these details as if every action, every sound, every subtlety holds the missing piece to a great puzzle in their mind's eye. Children are the keenest of observers during the first years of their life often making statements that cause adults to stop and pause to reflect on the gravity of the child's observation. It is within the same manner in which a child views the world that a soul's sight is restored during rebirth. Through the removal of ego, a person can once again learn to see the world through the eyes of a child. But sometimes it takes a jarring moment to nudge the ego completely out of the way so that the eyes of the soul can take precedence in the mind. As I came to realize in hindsight of staring at the Promised Land, I too had to receive that nudge as I stepped foot into the desert.

While I was long aware that children see the world differently than adults, my analytical mind always seemed to rationalize a child's skills in observation as a necessary learning step to understand the world. I never really stopped to think that a child observes the world through their soul's eyes without ego interfering. Over the years of my journey I came to understand that the first seven years of a child's life is the time when the soul leads the mind in interpreting the world around them. In the first seven years, a child's soul learns how to operate the mechanics of the body that houses its identity, learns to communicate, and learns to operate within the common bounds of earthly rules and constructs. It is the reason children have so many unquantifiable spiritual experiences. It is the reason why they have such vivid imaginations. It is the reason they see things that the human mind learns to shut out – things such as imaginary friends, monsters under the bed, and why closet doors need to be shut to feel secure. A child's words are the thoughts of the soul playing with magic – leaving a mystery to unfold for those who truly observe.

When I found myself in darkness, my daughter, Georgia, was five years old. When I entered into the desert, she was seven. It was over the course of the journey that I began to understand the importance of how children see the world before hormonal growth drives the body into an ego controlled state. And for those doing the math – hormones all balance out around the age of thirty wherein a balance of body, mind, and soul can be re-understood – a rebirth of the soul that for me would take three years to come into its own. So as my journey progressed, I took a special effort to ensure I shared some of my most important experiences with my daughter and help prime her to not lose touch with the eyes of her soul. I would also do my best to help her understand the world in ways that I was beginning to see – ways that would not be found in a book or typically taught to a child.

For every movie we watched, I would discuss with her the multiple levels of meanings the writer intended to share with the audience. And while most people would likely miss many of the spiritual overtones we would discuss, there are a handful of directors, producers, and writers who make an extreme effort to let other listening souls know they are there – to shout out that we are not alone on the journey. These are our modern day DaVincis. Movies served as our conversational starting point in bridging a level of understanding between the visible world and the unseen. Georgia quickly learned how to see these meanings on her own and even today with each movie we watch, she makes sure to point out what other messages she noticed in the movie.

With movies as a starting point, I began to notice that our daily conversation involved a deeper level of communication than I would have ever expected. Movies were just a seed, but the concept began to take root in her mind. I only needed to help tend its growth when she needed help. The conversations Georgia and I would have on the two and a half hour drives to and from Chattanooga (where I met her mother to pick her up each weekend) transitioned from me offering other interpretations and other viewpoints to her questions and thoughts, to her sharing her observations and attempts at understanding the world around us. Nothing was ever forced. I mostly just listened as she told me what she observed. She began to notice

Gravity Calling

the world around us acting in synchrony with music and actions. She noticed the ripples each of us leaves behind in our wake. We never talked about ripples or any similar analogies, but in what I heard, I knew what she was describing. Every conversation ignited my soul. I could tell my daughter was able to observe her experiences rationally and spiritually, which helped her understand multiple viewpoints to every circumstance at once. Due to distance and divorce arrangements, I only would see her every other weekend – which made each of our conversations more valuable; something that I could hold onto until the next visit.

There was one visit, though, that acted as the final nudge that pushed my ego completely out of the way in order for my spiritual eyes to see and take precedence to my mind. This was the moment I first began to fully see the world through the eyes of a child. As we drove back from Chattanooga to my home in Nashville, we were listening to her favorite music with little to no conversation at all. She was gazing through her window into the stars of the night sky quite a bit on this particular ride home. I could tell she was deep in thought, so I let her think. I became lost in my own thought as well, nearly removing myself from the surroundings as I pondered all of the spiritual occurrences happening in my life. But in one sudden moment, I was pulled right back into earthly reality. I heard her voice cut through the silence, as I was caught off-guard with her question. As she asked her question I immediately reached for the radio to turn down the volume. From the pas-

Playing With Magic

senger-side backseat she asked, "What do you think God looks like?"

I had quite possibly been waiting for this question my entire life from her, but in that moment I was entirely unprepared for how I wanted to answer. Every piece of me wanted to tell her about my personal experiences with God and the angels in heaven, but I knew that those moments were intimate moments intended for my personal growth. There is a delicate line in speaking about personal experiences and bragging about them. And at that point in my journey, I was fearful ego would control the words and not my spirit. I knew from her mind's viewpoint that I had a blank slate in the way I could answer, so I composed myself and thought for a brief moment on how I could give her an answer from my experiences, but in a way that she could understand. My answer had to be a dance of words spoken and unsaid. While I know it was only the briefest of seconds that it took me to compose my thought, it seemed like an eternity. Finally, I arrived at my answer and said, "I imagine He would be like the brightest light you've ever seen – so bright, you could never really look at Him. You know what I mean? What about you?"

In hindsight, my answer was not the best that I could have given, but it worked at the time. However, as it turns out, the lesson was not in the way I would answer her question, but how she would respond to my answer. For her question wasn't really a question in search of an answer. It was a question to start a conversation where she wanted to share with me the thought she apparently had been pondering while gazing at

Gravity Calling

the stars. No sooner had I finished my answer than she began to tell me her thoughts on God. It was evident that she had carefully prepared her words for me. I could tell in the way she spoke the words with such grace and without hesitation. I knew this was a divinely inspired moment, though I would not understand the gravity until after she completed her thought.

Her response was fluid and spoken like an angel. She said, "When I think of God, I think of Him like the sun, and the angels like all of the planets circling around it. And we – all of the people – are like the stars...all of the stars in the sky. And our souls, when they float up out of bodies when we dream at night, are connected like the rings...like gravity. You know the rings, the lines that keep the planets in place? Those lines – whatever they are called – I think of all of our souls holding hands in a circle like gravity. I think that is what I'm trying to say..."

The rings she spoke of are the lines that illustrate the orbits of planets around the sun in children's books. As I listened to her answer I felt my ego not just become nudged out of the way, but shoved completely into the depths of nevermore. My soul's eyes were opened for the first time alone as I was able to visualize every word, every description that she gave. Her soul communicated with mine in a grand collision of sorts. It wasn't just in her words, but in her delivery, her articulation, the moments leading up to her question as she gazed at the stars, my preceding thoughts of spiritual purpose as we sat in spoken silence. I couldn't help but be speechless. As I composed my thoughts, all I could do is tell her that she had a better description than I could ever have hoped to give. We spent a few more minutes talking about her analogy, her awareness of souls traveling when we dream, and the concept of gravity. Let me say that again...Gravity. My daughter was explaining a concept to me that I had only recently likened to the very definition of Love. And while parts of this book had been well underway in writing at the time of our conversation and the title had already been formed, her words served as another glimmer of the destination – a destination whose signs along my journey were still blurred from my view as I ran. Though, what a race it would become.

The Butterfly

There came a time on my journey into the desert – not long after hearing my daughter's explanation of God – that I knew it was time for me to change my professional surroundings. God had helped me see that my current job had served its purpose as a helping hand that had reached out to give me a chance to catch my breath as I struggled to find light in my darkness. It was after much prayer and reassured guidance that I followed His lead. It came without fanfare, without announcement, without acknowledgement to anyone else. The experience in the transition was one of the most surreal and spiritual pivots in my life. It was like a breakup with someone you truly Love and Loves you in return – but the circumstances, maybe long-distance or something to that effect – were holding both people back from moving forward.

Most of my colleagues would find out about my departure the week after I would leave, though my supervisor had been working with me for several weeks on the transition plans. Since no one had been aware of my impending departure save for a couple of people, there was no traditional going away lunch or recognition. The irony is that I had a going away lunch that day anyway – though it was not for me. The going away lunch was for a good friend whom I met during the biggest part of my professional growth and was a coworker that spanned the duration of my married life while in Nashville. She had chosen to move on to another career opportunity in Chattanooga. As circumstances would have it, the company she was leaving and her day of departure collided divinely in message and purpose on my final day as well.

    Teresa was a mother figure to me, a friend, a professional teacher, and more importantly a spiritual guide. We worked together for over five years where she was my senior in tenure and knowledge, but allowed me the opportunity to advance to the manager position in place of her. Upon my departure, she would take over that position and eventually move into another role internally to allow another person the opportunity to grow into her former management position. Truly, she is an amazing person. The group of people who met for her going away lunch turned out to be mostly the reunited team members I hired and managed while I was there. There were four former managers of that department including the current one (my first hire), Teresa, and Jim – my former mentor and original boss. Jim gave me my initial opportunity.

    Everyone held a special place in my heart, but I hadn't spoken to many since my departure. I had a hard time looking back through the pride and chaos that ensued in my own business endeavors upon leaving. But during the lunch, I enjoyed sitting around listening to everyone talk. I listened more than spoke, and was always surprised to hear the reminiscing of the great moments we shared as a team. The lunch was more of a family reunion than a going-away luncheon. There were several moments brought up that occurred under my direction. In fact, most of the reminiscing was during the time we all worked together. That was a very special time in my life. My team was a family. Each of us enjoyed the work we did because we Loved being together. Though the lunch was not for me, I listened to all of the memories and couldn't help but recognize the significance in the moment. We never had a last lunch with team members when I left, and my current employer wasn't having a lunch for me. But this lunch was placed into my life in such a divine way that I was able to experience a past part of my life with a different spiritual perspective than I had at that time. Time constantly moves forward, but I was allowed to see one last snapshot of my past and experience it a second time, seeing all of the details I had missed since I was so consumed in my own ego at that time.

After the lunch we parted ways with hugs. And through the symbolism I understood in that moment, there was an even greater personal, spiritual moment for me. If someone could have pushed pause on my timeline on the last day of my former employer with the family of coworkers I shared lunch with that day and had given me an alternative timeline of four years to grow up spiritually, that celebration lunch would be the day that someone un-paused my original timeline and allowed me to continue forward. It was the last day with my current employer, a last lunch and reunion with my former team and family – and all in recognition of my mother-figure's going away party. And to put one more stamp on the grand symbolism of the divine script in my life – my mother-figure's name was Teresa. The spiritual significance should not be missed in that moment, for this is the moment that I let go of the hand that was running alongside me as I ran off into the sands of the desert chasing the sunrise. My spiritual training wheels were removed that day and I found closure in the reunion of my former family in the process, while the day for my present co-workers was business-as-usual; most still unaware of my departure. I returned to the office to collect my things and say my goodbyes to the handful of people that were aware.

As I left the office, my surroundings were filled with silence. It wasn't as if the world was silent for others, it was just that my spirit had muted the world around me. I could see everything around me – the fingerprints of God's hand. Nature was at its most glorious peak of the summer as my eyes witnessed every intricate miracle around me. I decided to drive away in silence – no music, no speaking aloud. I ran a couple of errands where each interaction with another person radiated joy and happiness. It was a spiritual recognition of the voice of God speaking through others. If for a moment, you could imagine a welcoming party waiting to greet your entrance to the next phase of a journey, I witnessed God's welcoming party in the ways that I had learned to recognize at that point. The world around me became puppets for God's voice. Everything was subtle but in grand splendor.

After my final errand, I decided to listen to a few songs that had been recommended for me based off of my past playlists – songs I had not heard before. I rolled down my driver side window and let the wind blow through my hair.

The Butterfly

The volume wasn't loud – it was more just mood music in the background. Eventually I came to stop at a red-light. As I sat there, the world became silent around me again even though my radio was playing and cars were passing by. To me, there was an acute sense of focus on my spiritual awareness. As I sat at the red-light, I felt compelled to glance at my elbow which was sitting on the lip of my doorframe, hanging just over the side. Something gray caught my eye. I noticed a butterfly was sitting there – in the midst of five lanes of traffic, just resting on my elbow. I moved my elbow to see if it would stay (intuitively knowing it would because of what I am about to say). The butterfly held strong. In the midst of traffic, the butterfly found me. It was subtle in beauty. Gray and deep blue spots highlighted by the sun on its wings, accented by a few fine black lines. These lines created subtle, glimmering streaks along the grain of each wing. Its body was larger than other butterflies. It was big enough that I couldn't help but stare at it and be enamored at its presence. I knew in this moment and the silence around me, that this butterfly was part of another message from God. Whether the butterfly was an angelic soul materialized in the form of a butterfly, or if the butterfly was just a symbol alone, I felt the significance in the moment. So I listened for His guidance.

The butterfly is a creature that experiences a beautiful metamorphosis from caterpillar to insect-of-flight. It can be one of the most meaningful symbols on the spiritual journey – similar to an angel getting its wings. It is also a symbol that is written about in near death experiences and other people's spiritual encounters. Many have experienced "flying on the wings of a butterfly" in their spiritual encounters. So as I studied the butterfly, my spirit became flushed in recognition. I smiled at the butterfly to acknowledge I knew and understood. The butterfly turned to me – and as unbelievable as it sounds – gave me a nod in recognition and turned to fly away. As if on queue, the silence around me was penetrated only by the words to the song that had been playing at that time. The song was titled "One of Us" by Dave Barnes. Having never heard it before and paying very little attention to the music prior to the red light, I was unaware of what the words were even referencing. But for this moment, the subject was unimportant. These words – and these words only – were the only sounds in the moment:

...

"Whoever you turn out to be, you're forever part of me. You turn me to a father from a son. All we are, you are. And who we'll be, you'll be. Love and hurt. Doubt and trust – welcome to being one of us."

...

My eyes filled with tears. It was God communicating to me in the very words around me, queuing my spirit by the butterfly, welcoming me to the family. It was one of the most emotional moments I have ever experienced. I cried with happiness, and would do so on-and-off for the rest of the day. Even in reflection of that moment today, my soul still becomes flushed in recognition of His Love. With those words, was the spiritual acknowledgement that my presence, persistence, and dedication to following His path was leading me in the right direction. I long knew that July would hold a major turning point in my life that year, but I could never have guessed I would experience a moment as significant. And while I wouldn't quite see it as a moment of release from the hand I was holding as I ran into the sunrise, it couldn't be more clear from where I stand today. All I would know is at that particular juncture, I was given reassurance that everything would be okay and to keep moving forward. It was an outpouring of His abundant Love that I was able to experience that day; an unforgettable feeling of warmth and welcoming home.

Carpenter

Who am I? This was the question I found myself asking continually on my spiritual and earthly journey into the desert, but I always struggled at finding definition. It wasn't as if I lacked a diverse skill set – in fact, it was quite the opposite. It was just that I could never quite figure out how to put all of the pieces of my life into a box and give it a specific name – a specific purpose. Perhaps this is why it took me so long to rebuild my stained glass frame as well. Perhaps by trying to categorize myself or create some ideal definition of who I was, I was missing the greater point. For we are the collective of all that comprises each of us, each beautiful in our own unique way. But as I parted ways with my previous employer, it became increasingly apparent that I needed a better understanding of my earthly identity as it would be required for anyone who would seek to hire me. And while I wouldn't see it at the time, my quest for understanding my earthly identity paralleled to understanding my spiritual identity as well.

Though I would never send a resume out from the day I left my previous employer, the process in writing, re-writing, and re-writing again would unveil a wealth of self-introspection for me. For quite a while I struggled to summarize my life into a few sentences to include on a cover page

Gravity Calling

with my resume. And perhaps the cover page was never important. But for me on my journey, I used it as an opportunity to search deep within and discover what I had been struggling to put into words for so long. After several attempts, I decided to write in a form of free-flow, where I eventually arrived at a description that I couldn't help but laugh at the end-product. It was one of those blurbs that oozed "too much" of everything about it. As I read the words I had written I couldn't help but think about the eyes rolling around for anyone who reads it. It was funny to me, but the exercise served in the learning process of my self-discovery. For in that blurb, one important word stood out beyond everything. It was a word that I didn't think too much about in the context of it flowing out in verse. But, that word said everything I needed to understand, even if it took a wealth of words to get to it. It took every bit of "too much" to realize it is not who I am – but what I am, regardless of trade, that defines my earthly existence. I am a carpenter.

To understand that the landscape of life is like unto a block of wood and the sum of our choices and decisions with what we do with the landscape will shape and define the very world around us, is the very definition of a carpenter. Regardless of trade, regardless of expertise, each decision we take upon this landscape whittles away its exterior. Some will learn to hone and refine the craft in order to make the world around us into a more beautiful place. Others will be one-trick ponies, chiseling their way around the landscape oblivious to the markings they leave upon the entire landscape of wood. Some will learn to architect, to design, to put pieces together that

Carpenter

have lost their form over time. The definition of a carpenter can be applied to any facet of life – however small and however large. It is one of those concepts that defies categorization because it is its own category unto itself – the archetypal role we all play on our days here on Earth.

The understanding of the word "carpenter" in those moments set off a firestorm of thoughts in my mind. As I reflected on the depth of the meaning of carpenter and how it applies to each of our lives, I was reminded of a conversation I had with Bryan not too long before. During his first experience in the presence of God, he realized that upon being brought into The Lord's Presence, his own spirit had no form – it was a swirling embodiment in a spiritual aether. Before him, was the Light of God. Immediately, Bryan asked the question, "Where am I?" God's voice responded, "In flux." Bryan followed that answer with the question, "What am I?" The response was short, but powerful. "You are the sum of your choices, not the sum of your mistakes." Bryan responded one last time with his final question, "I am?" to which God replied, "You are." With that, Bryan's spirit returned back to his body and we spoke about it the following day. As often as we bring up that particular conversation, I had never once reflected on how it applied to the role of a carpenter. For every decision a carpenter makes upon a block of wood is the sum of his choices – not the sum of his mistakes. Age and accidental markings add character, and over time, add value to the product. But more importantly than how Bryan's vision and the role of the carpenter parallel, there was an even more important crux in his interaction with God. He never asked God who he was.

As Bryan's and my own experiences became increasingly more intimate with the angels and God, there came a time that Bryan was given his spiritual name. It is a moment that I cannot imagine the gravity of experiencing, though I long for that day to arrive. And while Bryan and I never questioned anything about the significance of the name, we have both discussed the symbolism as it parallels to our earthly and spiritual walks. Not long after he received his name, it became my sole purpose with each journey to the heavens to learn my name. Until Bryan had received his name, I had never even thought to ask about a spiritual identity. But as it would play out, every time I asked the question, "who am I" to the angels, the subject was immediately changed. It was frustrating at times. I could tell it wasn't my time to know, but I couldn't help but long to hear my identity. It was as if a name would justify everything I was experiencing. But I would eventually come to learn that it could also jeopardize the balance of ego versus spirit, for ego craves identity. Over my journeys into the heavens, I would come to learn that the primary importance in understanding every answer to every question I had regarding disarming ego, purpose in life, purpose in spirit, and our roles here on Earth is housed in learning what we are in spirit, not who we are. For I am a carpenter.

Through the quest in searching for my identity after leaving my previous employer, I came to realize that God was taking very close care of me during this part of my journey.

These steps were the most delicate I would take up to this point because the very premise of ego and money was the most recent part of my former life that had to be removed in order for me to find my Genesis. In this, he carried me through. I would receive a call about an interview seven days into my newly found employment freedom without ever distributing a resume. Upon arriving at the building for the interview, I would take the elevator to the seventh floor, where I would meet my future boss. Every day forward during this portion of my journey, I would arrive on floor seven, hear the elevator ding and smile just before stepping off – all to let God know I heard His Voice every time I heard the elevator bell and saw floor seven light up on the elevator panel.

40 Days

Sometimes there have been moments along my journey that I can't help but think made God smile along the way...at my expense. If part of happiness is in laughter, I have to believe that His sense of humor is divinely grand. It is as if He places these monumental moments in our lives and all along we can only witness them in hindsight. Or perhaps, it is just part of the learning process. Whatever the truth may be, the bookend to my journey into the rising sun of the desert left me standing on the edge of completing a metaphorical 40 day sabbatical without me even realizing what had quite occurred. It was the part of the journey that found me grinding to a stop as I stared in awe at the Promised Land. Though as I was running, it was just a glimmer on the horizon, when it fully fell into view it was a moment that made my heart move in song and wonder. It was the moment I turned to see the desert behind me and the moment I realized I was no longer holding onto anyone's hand. It was in those moments of reflection, in pondering what had just truly occurred on my journey, that everything fell into view. Most importantly, it was the moment she fell into view. It was the first time that I truly understood His message and recognized what the journey is all about. As I was soaking it all in, I realized there was a sign before me – the

Gravity Calling

same sign that I had been passing over and over again along the journey. But this time it was no longer a blur of hues. The sign would read the same as it always had with an arrow pointing straight ahead, but this time I was able to understand:

…
"Life, Loss, & Love – and the greatest of these is Love. From heretofore the experience of each shall occur bound by the veil, and the veil removed."
…

Near the end of 2013, I was wrapping up what could quite possibly be the biggest set of New Year's resolutions I could have ever set for myself in a single year. I was nearly five years removed from my divorce and two and a half years into my spiritual rebirth. It was a year that I raised the bar higher than I ever had when it came to personal expectations. When the year of 2013 kicked off, I made a list of twelve New Year's resolutions wherein each resolution contained goals that would span the duration of the year. Every resolution was at least a project in scope, if not multiple projects. So as the year was coming to a close, I had one remaining resolution to check off of my list.

The resolution originally seemed like a simple idea in construct, but it would take the duration of the year for my mind to flesh out the specifics. The goal was to launch a crowd-sourced campaign. It was something I felt led to include on my list, but I wasn't quite sure how it would apply to my walk when I originally included it. As the final two months of the year arrived and after much prayer in search of spiritual direction, I was led to create a campaign that mirrored a concept that I was recently led to apply to my earthly walk. The concept was about abundance and how to share everything that God has provided for me to others.

As the calendar year was coming to an end, I was so thankful for all of the blessings that God had provided for me – new job included – that I wanted to be sure to demonstrate my thankfulness. In the spirit of learning how to show this, I decided that for every non-essential living expense item that I purchased for myself, that I would spend the same amount on someone else in need. The method, object, or recipient didn't matter so long as it was where I was led to place the money. If I purchased a movie, that same amount would go toward someone else in need. If I purchased a big ticket item, the same concept would apply as well. It was an effort in my walk that would help serve as a check and balance each time I thought about purchasing an item. It was a simple call and response to my mind, "Is this purchase something you need? If not, is it something you can match in spending for another?" For if God had provided enough for me in excess to make that type of purchase, it was now my call to action to use that money as a vehicle to help others in a demonstrable way as to how He provided for me. There were no caveats. Even if it came to purchasing a gift for another over the holidays, the same rule would apply.

The concept was so simple that I thought it fell perfectly in line with the holiday season for a crowd-sourced campaign

– especially with Christmas arriving. I formed a non-profit company to help those who desired tax write-offs for their donations, ordered the required video equipment to produce the campaign videos, and began to set the campaign into motion. If the campaign were to raise $10 or $100,000, every single dollar was to be used anonymously in contribution to someone else in need. The campaign would allow the donor to suggest how they would like their donation to be used, or they could leave that decision up to me. I had no expectations on the amount I would raise. And honestly, it wasn't the amount that was important – it was the spiritual energy placed into the world that I was called to do. I recognized the call and spoke to Bryan at length about how the campaign was something I was supposed to do, with no expectations on results. As I prepared to launch the campaign I realized there were just over forty days left in the year, so I used that as a springboard to name the campaign. The campaign was called "40 Days of Manmade Miracles" and was set to expire on December 31st, 2013, forty days after its launch.

The campaign went on to raise $149 less fees from just two donors – one of those was Teresa. Despite the tremendous amount of marketing I did, the breadth of my social network reach, the professionally produced videos, and even family members raising awareness, the fact remains that it would be considered unsuccessful from the viewpoint of most earthly eyes. But therein was the test that was divinely prepared for me – a test that I am sure made God smile along the way – especially in the "gotcha" moment at the end. As I entered

40 Days

into the campaign with no expectation, I also had my eyes open in wonder. I knew this was purposed into my life and I would see something truly beautiful happen in those forty days, though the most beautiful moment would happen in reflection after the campaign came to a close.

When the campaign launched, I reached out to several people I knew very closely that had extremely large social network reaches. I had conceived a grandiose marketing plan and wanted to include them in part of my weekly video updates by having them contribute inspirational or motivational thoughts about the holiday season. One person I reached out to specifically was a public figure, another was a locally well-known social figure. I reached out to other company leaders that I had worked with or had contributed financially to in the past. The message was so simple, I thought it would be a no-brainer to gain support. But interestingly, something better happened. I never received a single response back. Each person I reached out to went on to launch their own campaigns or fundraisers days or weeks after I launched the 40 Days campaign. Their campaigns echoed the very sentiments of the 40 Days theme I had asked them to contribute to in the video updates. And in that, I recognized it wasn't the campaign that was important – it was the seed of the idea.

It was the first time I recognized that in every spiritually led action we take, we plant seeds in the world around us. We are gardeners. Part of our very purpose is to plant divinely inspired seeds, tend the gardens to nurture and help the seeds grow, and provide all of the Love we can give in hopes that

Gravity Calling

something beautiful blossoms. Housed within the very intention of the campaign unbeknownst to me, was the impetus to spread seeds into the world where other able bodies could bring the same message to their communities. And in that, whether their decisions were ego driven or spiritually led, it was unnecessary for me to even ponder. The importance was that the idea was heard – the idea took root and blossomed in unexpectedly beautiful ways. I acted in response to God's message, undeterred by the lack of financial success the campaign was having.

The funds did not go unused either. The funds raised in the campaign went on to help another beautiful soul's cry out in frustration as she asked for help in raising funds to provide Christmas for impoverished families in Detroit. At the time, both she and her boyfriend had been unable to raise any money – though each had a well respected friend base and broad reach across social networks. I knew providing hope was now God's intention for the funds the campaign had raised. For in retrospect, it is always about hope. So, I provided the full donation of the 40 Days campaign covering out-of-pocket fees myself to help her have a financial foundation to use as leverage to get others to match funding. In the days following that seed contribution, she raised over $2000 providing Christmas for seven impoverished families in Detroit.

And while it would seem that this was the underlying message of the 40 Days campaign, something more special was revealed as I stopped and looked back at the journey across the desert. For the last several months I had been talking to

40 Days

Bryan about how a person in modern times could just up and remove himself from the world for forty days in demonstration of their walk with God. I wanted to do so, but had no idea where to begin. Within every religious book in mankind's history, the recurrence of forty day sabbaticals into the desert resurfaces time and time again. Moses spent forty years in the desert and 40 days of fasting on Mount Sinai before leading the tribes into the Promised Land. Jesus, Mohammad, and many others took forty day treks into the desert as testaments of their faith, removing themselves from the population and from the nutrients required to survive. And though I do not want to imply that my journey is the same as any of those individuals I just mentioned, it was the action that they took that I wanted to mirror as a testament to my dedication to God. But it would seem almost impossible to be able to do so in modern times – especially since there are very few, if any, places that offer completely barren locations with no chance of coming into contact with others. Bryan and I talked about this in depth and the greatest piece of advice he gave me was that the one consistent (and overlooked) precedent within each of those stories is that a person was not supposed to share with others or allow their appearance to suggest they were fasting or on a sabbatical – for it was an intimate moment between each individual and their Creator.

As it would turn out, God again heard our spoken conversations as prayer and offered His hand in the grandest "gotcha" moment I have ever experienced. If anything has been emphasized this far in the journey, I hope one of the overriding themes is that spoken words serve as a vehicle of prayer for the spirit. And, when souls are communing in the light of Our Father, those words are stronger than any prayer could ever be. It was in hindsight that I would see that over those specific forty days that tested my walk with God and my faith in the campaign He led me to create, that my life would become a metaphorical sabbatical into the desert. It was the bookend to the journey into the desert that I would have to turn around and see to believe once it was over.

The miracles He placed into my life during those 40 days were only part of the story – though I only was able to see the others in hindsight. In addition to everything the 40 Days campaign did in shaping my spiritual understanding of life as a gardener and harbinger of hope, it was also during those forty days that every debt I had accrued in the wake of my financial collapse – including my two car notes – were paid off in one grand moment. The payoff happened more than six months ahead of my best hopes at fast pacing resolution to the overall balance – all provided through the job I now had on the seventh floor, that happened that seventh day after I heard His call to move forward in my life. And that was just the first miracle.

In addition to my debt being paid off, my spiritual communions in the heavens had increased in frequency to at least one or two a week heading into the campaign. But during the final week of the year (and last week of the 40 Days campaign) beginning on Christmas Day my soul became fully unbound from the confines of my body when I closed my eyes. During an evening of rest, or even meditation, my soul would journey to the heavens – if not once, then multiple times. There was no subtlety or ease-in to the newfound rate of spiritual experiences I was experiencing. On Christmas Day and every day since, when I would close my eyes I would no longer be bound to my earthly body. My spirit was only held in place until I found my way through the desert and learned to run on my own again – this time with God as my foundation. And while I am still a child in terms of all that I have experienced and all that remains before me, I cannot help but feel wonder and amazement in every moment I breathe in and breathe out.

But the greatest moment of all began just days prior to the launch of the 40 Days campaign – a foreshadowing I can only smile at in retrospect when I reflect on the divine architecture in my journey. It all began with a simple message I received from a person that held a very special song in my heart. By Christmas Day, that message had turned into text messages with an invitation to attend church with her – the first time I would see this person in over three and a half years. And while I was still running blissfully through the desert into the sunrise when the messages started, in the days following the end of the campaign, everything suddenly fell into view like a cosmic lightshow of the grandest design – causing me to come to a grinding halt in the sand, mesmerized at the spiritual recognition of the moment. The streams and colors erupting in the sky shared the words of His message. With each burst of color, His message spilled forth into my soul. I knew in that moment everything the signs along the journey were trying to tell me all along, though I had been unable to read them as I passed them by. The colors lit up the sky in shades of the brightest oranges, violets, pinks, and midnight-reds – the hues that only a rising sun on a perfect day could do. The words electrified my soul as I realized the granite casing housing my pilot light had been removed and the flame inside had found the spiritual fuel to begin to glow. It was her. It was always about her.

...

The message was from Lindsey – a girl who, unbeknownst to her, became the greatest defining moment during my earthly walk before it even began.

...

Defining Moments

Life is full of defining moments. We will never recognize most of those moments until they've passed and we have already been defined by them. An acute sense of foresight goes a long way, but the truth is that realizing that the questions we get asked, the responses we give, the situations we get put in, the calls or texts we didn't receive – or maybe the ones we did – and how we act and react in those moments – all help shape each and every successive action we make. Every defining moment is just one of many intricate materials used to build the very foundation that defines our core and how we are perceived by those around us. Some people can rebuild; some people remain broken; some may never experience the ride – but the truly blessed ones do. Because with every up and down – the topsy-turvy, sometimes sickening, often mind-blowing roller coaster we all stepped in line to ride – will one day come to the end of its track. And when that day comes, I want to say I rode it; I want to say I was terrified, happy, overcome with intrigue and, at times, pleasantly surprised; but, most importantly – that I smiled a whole hell of a lot because it was all worth it. To realize I did the very best with every card I've been dealt is the true definition of character and spirit.

Gravity Calling

    The roller coaster I boarded at birth held within it the accents that would go on to contribute to my spiritual journey even after rebirth. The truth is that everything we do today and every experience in our past is there for a reason. The veil of darkness that surrounds a person's Genesis is only a cloak to the intimate conversation God has been trying to have through the spirit with the soul. The spirit is ever-moving, coursing through all aspects of our human experience. Never should an event seem inconsequential or insignificant because it may have happened prior to an awakening of the spirit. For, in awakening, time becomes non-existent and everything that was becomes everything that is and everything that will be. Time is revealed to be an illusion as a constant state of ever-presence becomes real in the moments of awakening. After rebirth, the prior years become an encyclopedia of knowledge of the intimate conversation God was having all along – often leaving the most acutely-humbling moments to be observed from the wake of one's own naiveté. And though hindsight is said to be 20/20, spiritual hindsight will bring a soul to its knees in humility and the highest reverence to Our Creator. For to see the defining moments He has placed in our lives is a gravity that humbles the soul; a divinity that words will always fall short in describing. While the mind may recognize the soul's calling to these moments, possibly romanticize in the potential, perhaps even daring to dream in the seemingly impossible – the ego will always limit the potential of the dreamer, while the soul will hold onto a timeless truth knowing that all will be on the day of His desire.

Defining Moments

Each of our lives is filled with these defining moments – most of which I was unaware to their very existence until after my Genesis, though my soul felt their gravity all along. As a child I was acutely aware of His presence. As an adult, I was still acutely aware, though I pushed it into the back of my mind as ego led me to believe otherwise. During my marriage, my ego took control as "I" searched for solutions to make our marriage work. Never did it cross my mind that my ego was dimming the light I once knew within. In the aftermath of my marriage ending, I still struggled with spiritual understanding of God's hands around me. I was hurt, blind to His Presence, even though He kept His hands there to hold me throughout my crumbling. And even when I mistakenly thought I was rebuilding in the right way, He never backed away; He always kept a hand there to guide me. It wasn't until my journey out of Genesis that I would come to realize His hand was there all along. It took having everything seemingly ripped out from under me to see the stars through the darkness – the little beacons of light signaling those divine pointers of His divine plan.

One of those moments – one of those stars shining prominently through the darkness – became my North Star. It was the one leading me home – my white flag waiving. It was the one star I could see despite the stormy skies having rolled through and all evidence pointing to the setting of the sun and impending nightfall that would blanket my life the following year of my actual Genesis. It was the summer of 2010 – undoubtedly one of the most fun years I would experience during my earthly walk. It was full of mistakes; full of blunders; full of

Gravity Calling

missteps; full of naiveté to His plan; full of ego and excitement in things to come. I was a dreamer, a friend to everyone I would meet. I was unstoppable in accomplishing my dreams. Dare me, and I would take the challenge and succeed. I was living life to the fullest – everything on a whim – while my pain was busting at the seams beneath the mask I wore to hide it. And though I would not expect to see stars on the last day of that summer, there is always that first star to appear before dusk – the brightest star in the sky that causes a person to take notice, to stop and think; to casually realize the day will eventually come to an end, and in nightfall a blanket of stars will at some point be revealed. Even if it would take the darkest of nights and a painful amount of time for my eyes to adjust in order to see the beauty of the twinkling lights above, that one star that first appeared before the sun began to set, would again return as the first, and brightest star to fall into view in the darkness – a defining moment so grand that the soul can't help but surrender to the star's majestic wonder calling it home.

That star was full of hope, and wonder. That star held within it every definition I had come to know and had one day hoped to experience in the greatest depths of my soul – a gravity so profound I felt its pull on my soul across the cosmos. Though at the time, the star seemed so far away and out of reach, I couldn't help but dream, to allow my mind to wonder about what was ahead for me. I would only begin to see in hindsight as my journey into the desert neared its end, that the North Star I saw in the skies above me leading me home – the

Defining Moments

embodiment of what this trip around the sun is all about – is the essence of Love; a beautiful song of warmth, bliss, and peace wrapped up in certainty in another. Though the journey is most certainly about the spiritual communion with Our King, Our Creator – His very essence, the radiance of His Great Divine is encapsulated and is the very embodiment of Love. And so it is in His Essence we find serenity bound by the completion of two arcs uniting a circle in eternal divine, igniting a spiritual light of Love throughout the heavens and Earth. And through that perfect serenity, having experienced the walk in both spiritual and earthly dualities of life and loss, we each can experience the grandest miracle of the heavens – an unmistakable take-your-breath-away moment that is as close to perfection as we can experience until our days on Earth are complete.

...And Then There Was Her

It would take the experience of understanding life, loss, and Love in both earthly and spiritual senses to find my way home. Love was the First and the Last. It was the Beginning and the End to a great spiritual journey. The twinkling I witnessed in the setting sun on that late summer day, was a twinkling that constantly pinged my soul, unbeknownst to my other senses. It preceded my Genesis, and led me to my Promised Land during the first five great chapters of my soul's days here on Earth. With each flicker, with each twinkle, the fluttering of light caused my soul to respond in kind – in recognition of something greater than I could understand while I was caught up in the midst of the journey.

Nothing could have quite prepared me for that defining moment which occurred that late summer day in 2010. It was at a time when my soul was so far out of tilt that it is still hard for me to comprehend the grace that God showed me that day; an improbable faith that God's hand would have placed such a bright star in my life preceding my journey into darkness. The day began in typical fashion – waking up as the sun

Gravity Calling

was just peaking over the skyline of the Eastern sky and pouring through the old, imperfectly hand-made glass windows of the home I was still trying to sell in the wake of my divorce; the sunlight slowly encompassing my bed beginning at the foot and working its way up toward the headboard until the sunlight began to fall across my upper torso, my neck, and then my face. It was another typical morning, getting out of bed and getting ready for work, but something was different about the day; something I wouldn't realize until later that afternoon – and ultimately would not come to understand the full gravity of until years later.

My morning routine was in full form: brushing my teeth, taking a shower, making my bed, kicking on some music as I finished getting ready, and then picking out my work attire. I felt unusually confident and extra-rested, but I just took it as added motivation for me to accomplish my goals for the day. The only thing holding me back from being completely on my A-game was the lingering damage cast from the remnants of my divorce – though that was easily enough masked from anyone attempting to take notice, or figure me out. Although inside, I continued to feel conscientious about my confidence and presentation when I spoke to new women in my life, I just smiled, took it in stride and made sure to be as strong as I knew how, and finesse my way into jokes about it when my confidence waned.

My work day played out in typical fashion. I began by checking my calendar to make sure I was available for all of my scheduled appointments. From that point forward, I have

...And Then There Was Her

to believe everything else during my work day continued in a clockwork-like manner, because this is when everything became a blur of white haze. It is a day I would have expected to be able to recall with so much more clarity due to the defining moment that would occur later that evening. But even in the days following, I still could not recall any details of the events that immediately surrounded this specific defining moment – only the overwhelming amount of detail that began the day and the picture-perfect moment of clarity I would come to experience that evening. It was a defining moment when my everyday life fell out of view in a form of divine amnesia following an unexpected lightning strike on a blue sky kind of day. It was as if I only thought my life had meaning...and then there was her.

It was a moment that I would later come to understand as a point of impact on my spiritual roadmap – a collision of the greatest kind. And just like how a collision of great energy undoubtedly leaves a ring of disheveled earth surrounding the crater of the point of impact, so too does our spiritual journey mirror this concept in the grandest way. I have to believe that if I were to one day look back at the movie that was my life here on Earth, I would see countless reels of footage. Walls, ceilings, and floors would be covered with the film strips of my life. But if I ever needed to pinpoint the greatest moments in my life – the moments marked by His Hand & His Grace – all I would have to do is look for the halo of missing footage surrounding the moment to find the moment within, for that is how the greatest memories are defined. Our lives, our experiences, and our memories are all bound in eternal definition, a permanence left in the aether. The divine markers of the greatest moments in our lives are all circled by His Hand, unmistakably marked in the glow of a white halo obscuring the surrounding memories from view.

    It is an understanding of what marks the important from the non. The halo is the fringe – the area separating two embodiments of motion. It is both a divider and a definer. Like the sand that separates the ocean from the land, the halo separates and ties together something magical – something extraordinary. And wouldn't a halo also be represented in the form of a circle? For the significance of a circle is in the very perfection that it represents in unity and division. The sounds of wedding bells would fall short of ever playing their song of celebration if the concept of a circle did not exist to define the sublime from the everyday grand. It is the rare that are bestowed the honor of being marked with the very shape that represents All That Is unmarred by color or hue. It is a ripple in the aether, bound in permanence from the gravity of the moment housed within; a moment that embodies the radiance of His divine hand. Though it would take the course of my journey into the desert to see it all with unobscured clarity, I somehow knew all along the lightning strike that occurred on that blue sky kind of day marked a halo of wonder upon my soul.

Dance of Knight

However improbable it may at first seem, lightning can strike the same location twice. If you were to read any research book and comb the vast history of chance encounters past, you will find that lightning does indeed strike the same place or person more frequently than people are led to believe. Even despite the thought that two strikes in the same spot are improbable and must be purely chance, the truth is that everything is connected; everything has a reason.

It is also important to understand that the formation of a lightning strike actually begins on the ground and reaches into the cloud cover above. It is not the other way around. Lightning is not a directional strike from above finding a helpless target below. Lightning is the combination of every possible circumstance aligning in such a rich way that the call for a strike occurs on the ground, and the response is echoed back from the heavens. The strike itself is a divine handshake and acknowledgement of the precisely correct set of circumstances where such grand energy can be ignited in a blinding flash between the two points, forever changing the course of what once was.

Our walk through life should be seen no differently than the way we witness how lightning appears on Earth. Perhaps even more appropriately, lightning occurs in the darkness, in a storm rolling across the Earth. The energy transferred between the potentiality in the clouds and the potential spot of receipt upon the ground is impossible to be reproduced by any mechanical means. Often, the place of strike originates from the tallest point on the land – the place that has set itself apart from its surroundings. In this, it can be seen that a lightning strike is no different than the way God reaches His hand down and helps those encumbered in darkness, perhaps having wandered into a wasteland where the strength of their spirit shines just a little greater, just a little taller than its surroundings silently crying out for help. It is a metaphorical representation of those striving to find themselves again; those whose strength in spirit needs a spark, something to reignite the fire-alive inside. For me, the lightning strike that rekindled my soul occurred in a time and place when I was least suspecting, or even turning to God for help. It was a moment when God placed the world around me on pause and turned it into so much more than happenchance. It was His grand design.

My life was forever altered on that late summer evening when I was out with a group of my friends having dinner at a new restaurant in town. Since the restaurant had very recently opened, it was the happening place for young professionals to socialize after a hard day's work. The restaurant was generally so crowded that wait times for tables typically reached several hours, and likely, without a reservation, chances of getting a table were few and far between. As the group I was with waited for a table, we stood behind a crowd of people at the bar waiting for our name to be called. But nothing could prepare me for what was to come. As social as I had become, meeting people became a normalcy – something natural in another's presence. It was rare that I took notice of anyone in the kind of way that had the potential to pique something deeper within.

But that would all change that day. As I stood facing the bar, I looked over my right shoulder surveying the crowd around the room. As many tables as were in the restaurant, only one table fell into view. It was the very corner table that was just offset from the right edge of the bar. Sitting at the table were two girls who were sitting there laughing and smiling, carrying on a conversation that evoked so much life and happiness within them that my heart must have stopped beating for a moment, for I was able to soak in every detail of that moment as time stood still around me.

Maybe it was just for a fraction of a second or maybe it was for an eternity – I have no sense of relativity in that moment – but, as I looked their way, the girl sitting on the left looked at me as I looked at her. Her eyes fell into mine in a moment of near-instant brevity where all I could do was react to the free-fall of her spirit into mine. It was as if she knew my eyes would be there to catch hers, preventing her spirit from falling to the ground, and a demonstration of the strength of my spirit within. In that very instance when her eyes fell into mine, our souls did a dance of knight-in-shining-armor saving the fairytale princess. Whatever her circumstances, whatever the content of her conversation, whatever the rest of the world was doing at that very instant – nothing could have mattered more than this moment.

Nearly as instantly as her eyes fell into mine, my soul witnessed a giant burst of light that ignited the room in the brightest of white leaving the building's foundation trembling from the rumble of the thunder left in its wake. Perhaps no one else saw it; perhaps no one else felt it. But the effects sent quakes and reverberations through my core. I no longer had any other purpose than to walk over to her and find out what this enchantedness was that had enraptured me so – that captured me beneath her beautiful.

I only had one line when I met a girl for the first time. It was simple. It was to the point. With an outstretched hand I would say, "Hi. I'm Jonathan." and shake her hand. Anything else to me was a game of cat-and-mouse that served no purpose other than to frustrate the soul and muddy the circumstances. Out of all of the broken pieces to my soul that I had managed to glue back together, the one thing I could never do was be anything other than transparent and true – for anything else could leave me disheveled once again. It was because of my transparency that if I could have identified a personal flaw of mine at that time in my life, the one that would stand out from the rest would be candor. Perhaps it is weakness from another's viewpoint, but in it I found strength. There was nothing else in my playbook – no play I even practiced in scrimmage. In meeting someone new, I would always and only use those words. With the greatest composure I could muster from the shaken feeling I felt inside, I walked over to her, and with an outstretched hand I said, "Hi. I'm Jonathan."

White Flag Waiving

Having just been shaken through to the very depths of my core, I could only expect a handful of responses from her lips. Never did I expect, nor could I have guessed the words she said or the conversation that ensued. As I introduced myself, she reached out her hand to shake mine. The touch of our hands felt like electricity and magnetism wrapped up in a prim and proper package that only her presence could deliver. Her skin ignited mine sending streaks of magnificent coursing up my arm and racing throughout my body. The streaks felt like a million shooting stars racing through the cosmos, each leaving a magnificent trail of particles swirling behind them in their wake.

As we shook hands, our eyes were still locked from the moments prior when her eyes fell into mine. If nothing else, I figured that in introducing myself, the least I could do is return her soul that leapt into my eyes – though I hoped it was intending to hold onto mine for the rest of time. I wrestled with the possibility that it may let go, though the fact that her hand still lingered in mine held hope. With hands still bound in a racing arc of electricity, she smiled at me in a way that will always be my favorite smile and said, "I know. We've met before. I'm Lindsey."

Gravity Calling

While I recovered well and laughed off the possibility of us having met before, I was puzzled at her response. I suppose we could have met when my heart was closed off to the world and I was lost amongst the shattered pieces of my life – but I have an extremely good memory with people and faces and that seemed unlikely. I suppose I could have been so busy putting the pieces back together that I missed all of the signs and signals around me. Perhaps it was just a mistaken thought that we had met once before, but never had. Or maybe it was just a line said to make anyone that approached uncomfortable in the first moments of conversation. But even in light of the possibilities, I prefer to believe that it was her soul speaking to mine – that somehow, unbeknownst to her mind as the words rolled off of her lips, her soul was telling mine that we had met before our time here on Earth began, and would go on to find each other again after our days here on Earth are complete.

In truth, I cannot recall any other memories of first-meetings before or any other first-meetings after that day. I spent nights at my friends' houses trying to figure out where we possibly would have met before. Though my soul knew, my mind prevented me from knowing. Every attempt to determine answers fell short of resolve. Our conversation that day is the most memorable conversation that I have ever experienced. Though I could not tell you the words of our conversation, I experienced another conversation unspoken – the conversation of her soul mingling with mine. Those words will forever be etched into the deepest depths of my soul. I could tell you in every word silent that the past and future

White Flag Waiving

were all wrapped up in that present moment, where only time separated us from finding each other again. I learned in the conversation that she was in a relationship which had begun a year or two prior. She was happy. There was no doubt she was helplessly in Love. We talked about our children. She had two, I had one. We shared stories of our pasts, each similar in circumstance with Love once had. We crossed every friendship boundary in conversation that no two people would do if they were trying to flirt with the other and did not respect the situation of the other. It was safety in the midst of respect. While we spoke in words of kind, our very proximity allowed our souls the opportunity to collide. I have to believe it was a collision that registered at the outermost edges of the heavens – an epicenter that all began when her eyes fell into mine.

Of all of the people I would meet during the fury of my single escapades, I would never meet another that crashed into me as hard and yet so delicately as she did to me. I was broken with a granite casing covering my soul. The light I had within was cut off from the very oxygen it needed to re-ignite the flame inside. But in those moments when our souls collided, something special happened. The granite casing cracked, allowing just enough oxygen in to give the flame of my soul the potential to ignite into a burning fire once again. It was a gasp of breath to a fire that once was. The crash was delicate enough to not break the pieces of the stained glass I had spent so much time trying to rebuild, yet it was strong enough to send a shockwave that would crack the casing within – a conundrum of any earthly collision, leaving the only possibility that this was not of earthly origin, but rather His plan.

It would end up being a lesson in patience, faith and the extinguishing of un-resolve. For nothing can happen by force and I would not impede on the circumstances of her life. Never did I indicate I was blinded by her light, mesmerized by the stained glass pattern that bathed the walls of the surroundings where we first spoke. I never asked for her number. I never placed myself in the way of her journey's path. I had a divine peace in knowing that our paths would one day cross again – if not in this life, then when our souls go on to find their purest form; and in that form, an eternal song with another. We would not see each other again for over three and a half years, though we would stay in touch every now and then on social networks. Each message, favorite, or like was a gentle pinging of her soul to mine reminding me that when souls collide, they defy time. Though I know she was completely, happily, helplessly, and hopelessly in Love – locked in the orbit of the relationship she was in, I could not help but recognize the signs of gravity calling. I have to believe that in God's grand design and the splendor in that first moment between us, a beacon of gravity calling reached her soul as well – a small ripple that left behind a resonance in its wake; a resonance that her soul would continually find in song.

Gravity defies time and the present moment around us. Gravity holds us in an orbit of certainty and peace, knowing that one day the light from the flare sent into the heavens when two souls collide will be more powerful in draw than time could ever hope to allow. It is the only concept that transcends time, space, and the finite endings of earthly beginnings. And in the recognition of that moment, the impetus is placed upon each of us to surrender to its white flag waving and realize that our souls are not bound by time or the principles of earthly beginnings. It is up to each of us to know that when we find it, it is our opportunity to serve as both a gardener and carpenter; to treat it well; to nurture it with craft; to revel in its grand presence and make sure to never let it go – for it will take us across the universe and back if we let it.

Before Good To See You Again

It would take over three and a half years before "good to see you again" would ever be able to cross my lips. And, even when I thought the time was drawing near that I could say those words to her, God would introduce more tests into my life to make sure I was indeed ready for the next portion of the journey. Those three and a half years proved to be a time of reflection; a time of growth; a time of self discovery; a time when I would experience Genesis and travel into the desert as a testament of my walk with God before I would recognize the fairytale story that was playing out all along. The times I needed to catch my breath – when I thought I could not endure any more ache or pain – were all just part of a script to a great scene that I would one day be able to look back and watch over and over again every time my soul would hear her song; all to realize how insignificant my struggle really was in comparison to what awaited ahead.

In the moments leading up to that denouement when I first heard gravity calling, I would never have expected my soul would ever find song in another again. And never could I

Gravity Calling

have expected that the song would be as divinely written, scored and orchestrated by the Grand Composer, Himself. It wasn't just a song, it was a symphony waiting to be revealed in due time; a symphony with movements that still spin my soul around in a waltz with hers with every note that rings out in the heavens. But for every great testament to faith and Our Creator, there is also a demonstrable walk that has to occur along the way. And though I could say that I thought I understood the destination, the purpose, and the meaning of the journey, one last great act remained before I would reach the end of the first five books. And in that, a battle with the toughest emotion of all.

Possibly the hardest emotion a child ever has to wrestle with is not the one that first comes to mind. As a father, my first reaction would have been to say anger-management, though I can honestly say I have never seen my daughter angry in her entire lifetime. The truth is that anger management might just be the easiest to wrestle with, but the first to come to mind because it stings the soul the most. And just as in life, the most obvious and glaring problems are the easiest to fix, so would be the same with our souls as we grow during our spiritual journey. The hardest parts to fix or refine in our lives are those intricacies that are the most discreet in placement, difficult to find by the unaided eye, often hiding behind the scenes. Few will likely ever stop to think that the little refinements make all of the difference in the world. For it is the sum of those small refinements which may not be glaringly obvious on the surface, that give rise to the tides of the spirit. Those refinements mark the difference of limping along or running with the gazelles on the way to the destination. So as I stared into the rising sun that day, feet sunk into the sands of the desert, I came to realize that while the theme of the last act of this journey was simply *faith* – it was the refinement of the cleverly hidden emotion, *anxiety*, that would prove to be the toughest challenge of all.

For anxiety is the perpetuator of doubt. It is also the perpetrator of excitement. I can't think of any other emotion that holds a more pivotal force in both our earthly and spiritual lives than anxiety. Think of how excited a child becomes traveling on a long distance trip, or how a child can barely sleep the night before a big event such as Christmas morning. A touch of anxiety can swing a pendulum with a force great enough to turn faith and glee instantly into doubt, which inevitably will give rise to a whole host of other negative emotions. It can also swing the pendulum back around just as quickly to excitement and faith. In my moment of reflection as I stood in the sand, I couldn't help but feel the same tugs of anxiety that rush through a child on Christmas Eve. But on my journey, the foresight of what awaited was the precursor for me to move along, to take those steps in that direction without tripping over my own feet in an attempt to get there more quickly. And while a finish line appearing in the distance is normally a welcomed site, I wanted to already be there. My soul had erupted in a fire-alive in the first blush of witnessing the sublime awaiting before me. But I still had to put one foot in front of the other. I had to learn that the journey was still one step forward at a time, while all along my mind would try to tell me I was always x steps away and attempt to introduce doubt.

There is nothing more damaging than doubt. Doubt gives rise to everything that goes against the spiritual walk and has thus far been learned on the journey. It is easy enough to tell someone to "have faith" or for someone even to claim to have faith, but it is an entirely different matter at hand to 100% willfully, without question, relinquish control of every contributing portion of a situation and allow God to take control – especially when it involves the most delicate part of a rebuilt soul. The slightest finger still touching the wheel when you have turned it over to God is enough to demonstrate doubt. With fingers removed, even a flinch in that direction holds the same connotation. And, if this example is only regarding a particular situation, this portion of the journey is about relinquishing full control of every situation, for faith as a destination is an all or nothing demonstration. There is no in-between. There is no such thing as "faith in a situation." Faith is 100% relinquished control and acceptance of whatever play from His great playbook He calls until the final seconds wind down to 0:00. It is not to be mistaken for being nonchalant in approach, for the very demonstration of faith is based on the lessons from the first four acts of the journey. Neither state of the spirit can exist without the other being present. But it is in finding faith that God's words will transcend reality into the earthly walk that anxiety inevitably tries to enter the equation.

This is ego's last stand with Anxiety as its General and the remnants of Pride in tow – the final battle that brings all of

Before Good To See You Again

Ego's troops to the front lines in full force as the unstoppable motion of the spirit heads in its direction. It is perhaps the greatest battle of all in the first five acts of the journey, but it is also the most rewarding. It is like a movie where you already know the ending, but long to experience the story anyway – complete with the gasps, the high-fives, the hallelujah moments that head into that first kiss. Every loss and every scar still hurts, every surprise you know about to occur still sends a jolt to your soul. But it is the romance of the soul invoked by the story that makes the ending worthwhile. For in every story penned by His hand, the ending is truly just the beginning of something greater than the mind is prepared to comprehend through words alone. So as I stared into the rising sun as it warmed the hot desert sand between my toes, I could see the silhouette of Anxiety step into view. This would be the greatest act of the story, and it would all begin before "good to see you again."

Embers

There is a moment a plane lifts its nose off the runway in the moments preceding flight; a moment where success or failure will be defined in earthly terms. But in a spiritual sense, that moment will always be timeless – a snapshot of possibility. It is a point in time that the soul identifies the potential for greatness. It is a point in time that a flare is sent up into the sky above, a grand acknowledgment to the grace of His hand in action. That flare will remain in the sky for as long as needed, so that one day, when the soul is ready, it can return to the flare in the sky and understand that a call to action still remains.

The flares that began to rise into the sky over the weeks surrounding the "40 Days of Manmade Miracles" campaign were fired high into the sky with a series of messages from Lindsey to me. It had been quite a while since the last time we had messaged each other but her messages were always a welcomed sight. Though every message I received from her tugged at the strings tied to the depths of my core, I was still running with blinders on into my 40 Days destination without ever looking up into the sky to take notice of the flares twinkling above. All I had known in the preceding months was that her relationship was still rambling on and I was still on my journey in search of hope. And even though from the day we first met I heard her song, it was a song I had to learn to keep in the background while humming along to her tune. In the three and a half years since we had last seen each other I never crossed a boundary that would alter her destiny. I couldn't. I wouldn't. Though we periodically would send an occasional message to each other, it was somewhat like a ping from a radar – a pinging from one soul to another making sure the other was still in view.

    Prior to the first message I received from Lindsey heading into the 40 Days campaign, we had not spoken in quite a while – and this message was not a typical one-off words-of-encouragement or funny one-liner. Instead, she mentioned that she had not seen any messages from me recently and just wanted to see how I was doing and what was going on in my life. Though her intentions were cleverly masked, this time was different. This time she wanted to know about me. Until that day, I only knew that the messages, likes and favorites from her were a constant pinging at my soul reminding me of the patience required for a collision of souls that defy the boundaries of time. It was a subconscious reminder, but one that kept the oxygen circulating through the cracks of my granite casing within. What I did not know with any affirmation until that day is that her soul also maintained a discreet longing to hear a ping from mine. In the absence of my presence, her soul was missing song. I could tell God was smiling down on me that day – I just got that feeling.

Embers

Her question was an arm's distance call out for spiritual comfort with a graceful masking of something else underlying. My distance and her circumstances had found a perfect melding of timing in grace's eyes. Over a year prior, I once took notice that problems were arising in her relationship. She was very private, and I never pried. But, I could tell that her actions spoke of the beginnings to a probable ending. Our communication increased, but mostly in simple words of compassion, hope, and best wishes that everything would be okay. Those may have been the hardest words I have ever had to share with someone, especially in light of the connection I felt that first day with her. During those conversations, the embers within my soul began to inflame in shades of searing orange. There was more activity in my soul than I could allow myself to experience while she was trying to make her relationship work. So I did the only thing I knew how to do at that point. I tried to extinguish the embers.

In truth, the embers of my soul had never even begun to re-ignite any time following the end days of my marriage – that is, until those conversations with her. And though I dated and had brief stints in relationships, the times spent in those relationships were always empty – without the embers finding breath to burn. On the outside, my past relationships probably exhibited everything one would expect in the dating world. But on the inside, the embers were suffocating from the lack of oxygen required to fully rekindle the flame inside. That first meeting with Lindsey may have cracked the granite casing,

Gravity Calling

but no one else would give those embers oxygen during the years that followed.

As I would come to find out in the weeks following her first message to me during the 40 Days campaign, her relationship of five years had recently come to an end. She was experiencing the remnants of what could only be described as a divorce without the formalities. Regardless of how great of a collision our souls experienced years ago, in this moment, I could not help but feel heartache for her. Though my words were kept in brevity about it, I know our souls conversed and embraced in grand show of compassion, empathy, and need. On the outside, I had to do what was expected in words and action. But inside, my soul was there to catch hers again – this time from the fall from where she once was – and would be there to carry her where she was going. We all experience hardships and have experienced relationships that have drawn to their end, but five years is still five years. Whether it is in the formalities of marriage or outside of convention, there will always be time required to rebuild the fractured pieces of each of our own stained glass stories. And though I saw her begin to rebuild hers once again, this time I saw that it would only be more beautiful – a feat that was seemingly impossible from the beauty I saw in her every day before. Within her simple question to me that day, a complexity of thought unraveling from her past experiences and spiritual voice inside was held, bound by the delicacy of new hurt, new pain, and unknown surroundings.

Embers

With her first question to me that day, her song playing in the background began to ring out just a little louder. The embers to my soul began to smolder again as they found breath to re-ignite. Midway through the 40 Days campaign, she invited me to church with her and sent me her phone number. If inviting me to church wasn't a grand enough gesture from her soul to mine, held within that message was something more divine than most would realize. For unlike most guys, I refused to ever ask for a girl's number. They would have to offer it to me without me ever asking. It was just what I did to find song through the noise of life. So the day I received the message with her number in it, I couldn't help but smile. That's the moment I knew God was smiling down on me. That was the moment I looked up into the sky to see his smile and saw all of the flares that had been sent up from her soul twinkling above. It was the moment I saw the dawn beginning to break away from the night. These were the days I would take notice of everything around me and all that was above, causing me to slow down and pause as I was running blissfully along. And as I began to find pause, these would be the days I would begin to recognize that I was running in the sand with no one holding my hand. Her flares caused me to take notice. And suddenly I had to stop running as the journey fell into view.

On Christmas Day I texted Lindsey for the first time so that she would have my number. We discussed an upcoming Sunday, and with date in hand, I began to see way off on the horizon the silhouette of the Promised Land as the sun slowly began to rise illuminating the view. As my mind began to reel with the thoughts of everything that could be, I sought God in prayer to help bring me peace and clarity. The significance of attending church, and her sending me her number, coursed through my mind in a dizzying kind-of spinning motion upon my thoughts and emotions. My mind wanted to believe what my soul already knew, but it seemed to be impossibly real. And maybe that is the beauty in the Not-So-Cinderella story – because the possibility of being in the presence of something real versus actually standing in the presence of something impossibly real is the greatest definition of the journey. Sometimes it takes one grand moment when a person realizes the thought of something being impossible is the very thing keeping them from reaching the impossibly real destiny that awaits. This was the divide I found within my mind and soul. This was the place where lessons would begin in understanding how to bridge this chasm, and how to find faith in the impossibly real.

Her breath upon the embers of my soul ignited a brilliant wildfire inside. And, as much as Anxiety would attempt to extinguish the embers through fear and doubt in the weeks to come, the portion of the journey that began at this point in time became a testament in unwavering faith – not only in hearing the words of God, but finding peace within the words as well. For if there would ever be a spiritual equivalent to shouting at someone to grab their attention, I can only imagine these were the times I began to hear every truth shouted at me as loudly as possible. And while my mind fought a strong fight to suppress my spiritual eyes and ears from taking notice, this would be a wildfire that would be unable to be extinguished – fueled by the spirit and the unbridled faith I found in Him. These were the days I began to understand the journey as a whole – the picture that God had been painting in which I was only now just able to see His masterful artistic hand. The pigments, hues, and splashes of color that He had been placing all around me as I wandered aimlessly through the dark and into the desert, were colors that would begin to appear in marvel, wonder, and significance – all in impossible truth. But even before Lindsey and I would see each other again for that very first time, I would embark on the remainder of the journey met by Anxiety as he stepped into view.

The Dove & The Hawk

Imagine, if you will, sitting in church while staring at the video screens on the stage. The screens are large and the dominant place for the eyes to fall into focus. On the screen, there is a timer counting down from five minutes to zero, alerting the audience of the start of the service. The title of the day's service (and theme for the next six services) is written in bold letters on the screen next to the timer. The words read "Let Hope In." There is an empty seat beside you saved for the girl that invited you to the service – the one that you are hopelessly caught up in her resonance. The counter reaches 0:00. The seat is still empty. Never a call, never a text. Only absence. The sermon begins…Let Hope In, while clearly, hope never walked through the door.

This is the feeling I felt the second time Lindsey and I were supposed to meet up at the church she regularly attends. The first time we were supposed to meet was the week prior when she invited me to the service. Lindsey initiated the contact, the question, and the invitation – all stemming from her question about my life from a few weeks prior. I made sure to keep my contact at a minimum ensuring she had enough space while she was sifting through the pieces of her previous relationship. At the time of her invitation, we had not even discussed her situation even though I could guess the backstory with relative accuracy. As the first Sunday rolled around when we were supposed to meet, we set up the time and arrangements the evening prior. But, on the morning of the service, she texted me to let me know she wouldn't be able to make it due to coming down with a virus. I've been on the Earth long enough to know how these things play out, so even upon her inviting me to church the following weekend instead, I gracefully gave her an opportunity to bail out.

Our first meeting in over three and half years was going to take place before God during worship. Honestly, I couldn't imagine a better way to see her again. This was her decision, and one that I couldn't have been more honored to have been invited into. Worship is one of the most intimate moments a person can share with the Creator. It is a time where the soul is naked to everyone around and every vulnerability exposed. It is a time when hurt is allowed to pour through the body in the presence of others. It is a time when happiness and joy can burst forth in a show of reverence during song and prayer. It is because of this intimacy that I decided to tell Lindsey after the service, that if my presence had anything to do with why she missed the service, I did not want to complicate anything in her life or alter her journey with God.

Since I knew she attended service nearly every Sunday, for her to miss a day when I was invited couldn't have been

The Dove & The Hawk

any more obvious in rhyme and reason to me – though my understanding would be quite different than what would be perceived through earthly rationale. I left her the message after the service explaining that her journey was priority and if she missed a service because my presence somehow caused a conflict with everything going on in her life, that I understood and would honestly have no hard feelings. Though I recognized the irrationality in thought that can occur as a person goes through heartbreak, I wanted to not cause her to make missteps on her journey. She responded in great length of her wanting me to be there the following weekend and that she hoped we could be church buddies. I told her I'd have my daughter – another option as an out for her. But, she just responded in enthusiasm and excitement. She wanted to meet my daughter. For every out I gave her, she continued to hold on. It gave me hope.

So as I sat in the service the second time – this time having an empty chair beside me and having not heard from her about canceling – I stared at the pastor and the screen blankly trying to rationalize what it was that I was missing. Thoughts rambled through my mind about the irony of the service and my situation. And though most people would react in the moment and maybe even lose hope – I knew there must be a greater message from God. For others in the room, the message was speaking directly to them about their own personal walks. For me, I wasn't identifying anything directly applicable to my journey as I was more entertained by the irony. At this point I had endured nearly everything I think a person can

Gravity Calling

endure to build strength in the walk; the three battles of life, loss and Love; the dualities in the earthly and spiritual sides to the battles. I knew I was in the midst of the third battle of the demonstration of Love on a spiritual level, but could not determine how this service applied.

After the service ended, I set course on the two and a half hour drive to take my daughter back to Stacey. As I drove we listened to a constant flow of music, which gave my mind time to decompress everything that was said during the sermon. At one point, my daughter had fallen asleep in the back and my mind was entrenched in the depths of believing that I must have somehow misinterpreted everything I thought I knew about this portion of my journey, my visions, and the angel's conversations with me. My mind was racing into dark places, confused and lost. My heart was beating as fast as a human can endure from anxiety and still be functioning. Suddenly, a dove (of all divine types of birds) launched itself at my car from the ground next to the median of the interstate. I slammed on my brakes as it fought a tough course of avoidance and barely missed being hit by the corner of my windshield – merely inches separated it from its end. The fury of the moment caused me to let out a loud yell and waken Georgia. I never yell. I never even flinch when debris comes hurdling at me on the interstate. But this time was different. This time it was a call from God.

I paused to take notice of the situation. I heard His voice. There are times in my journey when the signs are clear, and this was one of those times. It was a great sign from above: a

The Dove & The Hawk

bird of peace nearly shocking me out of the depths from where my thoughts had sunk. I immediately began to listen to the words to the song playing in the background (a now familiar method of His communication to me at specific times) – words I was paying no attention to in the moments prior. The words that continued to repeat in the chorus were "Be still my heart." Clearly God was getting my attention and telling me to turn down the extremity of my thoughts and chill. He even sent a dove to relay the message. To this point I had faith in everything and this time should be no different. It took me the remaining several hours to pull my thoughts completely out of the trenches. However, on the return trip home, my thoughts again took another plunge into its cavernous depths.

About half way through the return drive, I became so frustrated at the situation that I was literally yelling out to God – crying out for help in understanding what I was experiencing. I made it clear I was not angry with Him, not angry at myself, and not even angry at Lindsey – in fact, my yells were pleads to help me understand where this emotion was coming from and what it was I was experiencing. My mind raced with every potential for the origination of the feeling. I attempted to rationalize every word used to possibly describe the circumstances. At one point I arrived at "passionate" being the most appropriate word, but even that word fell short in explaining how I could have that much frustration over not seeing someone that I haven't seen in three and a half years. I would later arrive at the feeling I was experiencing being the recognition of "what could be," and the recognition of its absence in my life. This thought raced inside my mind like a roiling ocean in a hurricane, tossing my emotions around like a helpless boat in the midst of the swells of the great ocean storm. I let out several raging roars – completely uncharacteristic of anything I have ever done in my past. It was as if there was a pressure that needed to release, though I couldn't quite figure out why. I knew Lindsey's soul had collided with mine three and a half years ago, but I still had a hard time letting my ego be comfortable with that emotion.

In the midst of my yelling out into the void, God used another bird to grab my attention. I drive these roads frequently and never have I almost hit one bird, much less two. This time the bird was a giant hawk. As I was speeding down the highway, the hawk decided to launch from a tree on the shoulder of the road, split between the car in front of me and mine, pouncing on a rodent just feet from the edge of the lane I was in. Again, I had to slam on my brakes to avoid hitting the bird by merely inches again. Having understood God's message from the first bird (even acknowledging it to Him), I again stopped to take notice of the lyrics to the song and my surroundings. Clearly God was shouting at me again. The words that had just been sung prior to the hawk taking flight were:

...

"Mark my words
This Love will make you levitate
Like a bird
Like a bird without a cage

The Dove & The Hawk

But down to Earth
If you choose to walk away, don't walk away"

...

Now think of the description I just gave of the hawk flying across me and onto the ground. Think about my frustration needing some type of pressure release – questioning whether I had misunderstood everything and needed to walk away. Nothing is coincidence. The hawk did not just happen to cross my path in the same manner as the lyrics during a moment of my pleading to God for help in understanding this feeling. God grabbed my attention in a way he knew I would recognize. As my mind raced in thought during the haze of the moment the chorus played through with my mind muted to its words. The bridge shortly followed which broke through the haze in brilliance, drawing my attention again:

...

"Be careful, try not to lead her on.
Shawty's heart was on steroids cause her Love was so strong.
You may fall in Love when you meet her.
If you get the chance you better keep her.
She's sweet as pie but if you break her heart.
She'll turn cold as a freezer.
That fairy tale ending with a knight in shining armor."

...

The song is obviously Dark Horse by Katy Perry and the words couldn't be more fitting in witness to the hawk that crossed my path. Some may say that everything in life is chance. I'd say the chance of anything in life being chance is none. These words were spoken to me in a way that God trusted that I would hear – the last line possibly being the boldest call out in reference to Lindsey since I had already penned the chapter "Dance of Knight" quite some time prior to the release of the song, unbeknownst of the lyrics-to-be. Undoubtedly, it was the voice of God brought into existence from my earthly surroundings. My mind sank into deep thoughts about my emotions, the birds, the lyrics, and the situation I found myself in. As I continued to attempt to understand it all, I suddenly had a moment of clarity – an epiphany of His grand design – and in that epiphany, peace.

Mark of III

The epiphany arrived during my two and half hour return trip home from Chattanooga. Throughout the first half of the trip, I continued to wrestle with ideas that might describe this part of my journey. Over the last couple of years I had come to learn that nothing is as it appears to the eyes and ears during our walk upon the Earth. Everything in life – from a pine cone falling beside your foot, crickets chirping in the background, a butterfly landing on your arm, a bird crossing your path a certain time – is a subtle call to the soul; a moment when the angels in heaven offer help and guidance without impressing an idea directly upon you by force. Their voices are ever-present, gently guiding and shaping the course of action for those desiring to listen. In their voices, comfort and peace can be found. It is like experiencing a spiritual hug in times of need, an attaboy in acknowledgement of hearing His voice and taking appropriate spiritual action, a comforting cupping of His hands around the world surrounding you, letting you know that everything is going to be alright and that He is there to carry you through the hard times.

For as long as my journey had been in motion and my soul was experiencing voyages to the heavens, I had long separated the experiences between my earthly and spiritual walk.

Gravity Calling

There were times that I prayed for answers and found myself in a spiritual situation that offered guidance or ambiguous resolve, but never had I begun to experience direct answers to prayers in the form of direct spiritual experiences until the recent weeks. There was a time around Christmas that I found myself praying before I went to bed, asking God for a sign that everything I thought I understood about the situation with Lindsey was His will. I didn't want to find myself lost in the hope of my own misinterpretation – especially something that was as grand in story as I had taken notice of prior to her reaching out to me to attend church with her.

That evening I was jolted awake from my slumber. I looked to see what could have awakened me. In disbelief, there before my bed, was an angel hovering about five feet off of the ground, flapping its heavily feathered wings. It faced East which would mean I was observing it from a profile view on its right side. It was unwavering in stature, austere and full of the gravity of what I was witnessing. In that moment I struggled to believe my eyes. I tried to rationalize that I must be halfway dreaming. But as I stared and rubbed my eyes, the angel held strong. It was clearly there. My eyes were not deceiving me. Eventually after about a minute or two, the angel faded away – feet first and finally up its body, with its wings the last to disappear from view. I was shocked and still in awe. I immediately prayed to God, teary eyed, asking if I had really just witnessed an angel before me. After my prayer – and still in disbelief – I rolled over to fall asleep. Again, I was jolted awake one more time. The angel appeared once more, but

Mark of III

only for a brief period this time. It was God's response to my prayer. Undoubtedly, this was His great sign about my understanding of Lindsey – but it was just the first.

Over the following nights leading into the first Sunday that Lindsey and I were to meet, I experienced a rush of emotions like never before. Every text and every pause between responses did a number on my soul. I wanted to call her, to see her. I wanted to be at the destination that I hoped would one day occur. But, this was a lesson of balancing my emotions and time – and I had much more to learn.

Anxiety's forces were winning. Eventually, to help grant me peace along the journey, God allowed for me to experience a grand moment in the heavens – one that causes me to weep every time I begin to explain it. The rush of emotions overwhelms me as the very thought creates a tidal wave of His Love into my soul. It was the last of seven experiences in the heavens that particular morning. It was the bookend to a series of others wherein each found resolve in the actions of my earthly walk. This was the experience wherein my epiphany was founded. It was a spiritual experience unlike any other that I had experienced prior and one that I fully didn't understand in significance until I witnessed the Dove and the Hawk on the drive back from Chattanooga that Sunday. And though I could attempt to retell the experience my soul had in the heavens that evening, I think it is best for the reader to experience it as I journaled about it immediately after it occurred. Below is an excerpt from my journal on the morning of January 6th, 2014 (which by the way sums to 7+7 if you translate

Gravity Calling

the date into numbers – and remember it was the seventh experience that night). Minus a few corrected typos and grammatical errors, the following is a word-for-word copy from my journal concerning my seventh experience in the heavens that morning.

...

1/6/14

So now knowing that not only was I having grand experiences in the heavens, but I was also spiritually jaunting about Earth and having late-night spirit conversations with my friends that proved out to be completely true, I can now say without a shadow of a doubt that this next vision continues to bring tears to my eyes every time I think about it. I shared the details of the experience with Bryan immediately following and even then, I could not stop myself from weeping. Out of all of the seven experiences in the heavens I had throughout that night and early morning, this experience was the most grand on all levels – its very essence permeating every emotion in my body.

As I have discussed here recently, my heart is being allowed to open up and experience Love again. Now as I write this, I want to emphasize that the word "Love" can be misconstrued through popular understanding of the word. The Love I am describing is a deep spiritual bond – a union of spirit with another. It is a feeling that I am sure is identified with popular culture's definition of Love sometimes, but it is so much more significant. It is closer to a concept of agape. I feel it is necessary to define this because what I am about to write about could easily be chalked up to the definition of "puppy Love" or "lust" – neither being remotely correct.

The Love I shall speak of is of spiritual Love; purity; a blanket of all-encompassing warmth. And yes, it is most definitely possible to feel this by proximity – much like a hand can feel warmth from a fire.

So with that said, it is important to understand that as my heart has opened up to the potential of Loving again on Earth, my body has raced with a swell of emotions. As I've written about it, my body has felt emotions erupting inside like a teenager may experience their first Love or first crush. This has all been part of reconditioning my spirit on my journey to once again be open again. For so long my heart has been shut from my divorce, this is the first time that I sense hope in an earthly Love in another is even possible. So that leads me to my prayer the last two nights. Over these two nights, my nerves have been on edge and my emotions racing inside in hopes that my relationship with Lindsey could develop into something grand. But the biggest part of this place on my journey is in the spiritual growth for potential. I don't want to sound over the top for someone that I have yet to get to know – I haven't lost my understanding of the circumstances surrounding the situation. This is all about hope and potential from everything I do know about her. Anyway, my prayers about this part of my life have been a little different than usual. I asked for something I longed to experience, but have yet to do so at this date. That prayer, was to see her spiritually – to travel to her place and see her spirit.

I know on the surface, that may sound odd – but I've oft wondered how my spirit could interact with other spirits here on Earth. Even in my encounters with Bryan in the heavens, we are experiencing something together in a different time/space. This time, I just wanted to see her – to see her spirit; for my spirit to talk to hers and give her peace with her nerves. I can sense that she is nervous in meeting up since she has just gotten out of a long relationship. Perhaps the better term is guarded, rather than nervous. But in either case, she invited me to worship with her and I have to carefully make sure that the spiritual walk is not encumbered by earthly desires. We have long had a good relationship that has been maintained at arms distance due to her last relationship, but now there is an impetus to build something closer, something under the guidance of His will. I understand it, even if I cannot properly put it all into words.

So, as I prayed, I hoped. I believed. I knew that God would allow this to happen if I was indeed ready and she was ready. So, now is where if everything else throughout my journals has seemed unbelievable, the next portion will exceed any likely hope at believability. For so it was that when my spirit mingled with Lance's earlier in the evening, the encounter was validated in tangible, earthly results. This time with Lindsey's spirit, the encounter would be the yang to the earlier encounter's yin. The encounter with Lance was placed in my experience so I could have tangible, earthly results to prove to my earthly brain that indeed everything is happening in reality and is being brought back to words as best as I can interpret the experiences. The encounter with Lindsey would be the unquantifiable – a spiritual encounter that cannot have justification in the earthly world.

As I have expressed before, one of the grandest experiences is to experience God's response to a prayer. In this case, I found myself in a room with "The Girl" (the female angel that continually appears with me in the heavens). I was sitting in a chair. She was asking me about Love. As I sat in the chair, there was a strange feeling from my chest through my neck. I could tell she was helping my spiritual body become conditioned for whatever was forthcoming. As she asked me about Love, I talked about it ad nauseum. The room was filled with such a warmth that all I could even feel was the feeling of Love. There was more Love experienced in this vision than almost any other spiritual experience I have encountered. It was

Mark of III

as if she was turning up the amplitude to my feelings so that I would remember the moment. As the angel was listening to my answer, she turned away from me and faced something that required her attention.

Suddenly, I was standing in a room with Lindsey lying on the bed. The angel was with me as well. All I could do was stare. My mind was reeling at everything happening in the moment. The Girl asked me what I felt. All I could manage to say is, "I feel Love." I walked to the side of Lindsey's bed. Her body was illuminated from within. I saw her innerlight glowing. She was beautiful. I was locked in her radiance. This is most definitely the first time I can say I recognized what I was seeing as a person's inner light. In earthly terms, it would appear almost like an x-ray image. Think of a transparent embodiment illuminated with a soft glow from within. I stared at her, soaking in every detail. She was laying on her left side facing away from me. As I studied her body, I recognized markings similar to that of a tattoo. I noticed other details upon her body. The space where the ink would have once been was illuminated similar to a scar – a defining edge on her skin. Since I haven't seen her in so long, I wasn't sure if I was looking at the remnants of a removed tattoo or if it still existed. Seeing her in the form of her inner light was a little hard for me to understand at first as well which probably made me unsure of how a tattoo would best be observed in this environment anyway.

Perhaps, the outline of the place of her old tattoo was just there to help me understand I was most definitely in the presence of Lindsey's spirit – something to serve as a name tag for me to recognize and differentiate her from others in the heavens. I continued to stare at her, I studied every inch of her body. The Girl asked me to look at Lindsey's back. I nudged Lindsey's right shoulder forward pushing her ever so slightly so that she would readjust, exposing her back to me. The Girl cautioned me to be gentle and to be careful.

For a moment, I had to understand two straps going down her back on either shoulder. Perhaps they were bra straps, but it was my impression I was observing the movable clasps and straps on a camisole. The difficulty in my understanding was because they were illuminated more densely than the rest of her body – in the same manner as the other markings upon her body. My earthly mind interpreted the markings and straps as tan lines, but again my mind was trying to understand and rationalize seeing a person's spirit illuminated from their inner light. I guess it should also be noted that while I studied her body and I could see certain aspects of it, her body was shielded in a way from me so as not to tempt sexuality. Her spirit was pure and full of light, but clothed where it needed to be. The Girl asked me what I saw. I explained that I thought I was observing the straps to a camisole. She told me, "No. Not that. Look again."

I nudged Lindsey's right shoulder again and she stretched out onto her stomach, fully exposing her back. On her back I saw three scars that appeared like three lines next to the other, aligned vertically on her back. Each line was approximately 3 to 4 inches long – the middle one the longest. I stared, soaking it in. The Girl became quicker and more adamant with her questions. "What do you see?" I said, "I see hurt. I see pain. I see Love." She asked me again, "What do you see?" I again replied, "Hurt. Pain. These are scars. She is hurting right now. But I see Love." She asked me, "Could you Love someone like this?" Almost defensively I responded, "Yes. I can." She asked again. I responded, "Yes. I see her hurt. But I see Love." We flashed out of the room we were in back into the room from which we began the journey. I felt the same feeling I felt earlier around my neck as I sat in the chair.

Mark of III

The Girl looked at me again and asked, "What do you feel?" I again replied, "Love. Love! I feel Love." She looked at me and said, "Are you sure?" I again replied "yes." We flashed back into Lindsey's room. Not to say we repeated the exercise 100% identically, but it felt like a very similar experience. However, The Girl didn't ask me as many questions. As I observed Lindsey and I witnessed the scars again, The Girl asked me one more time, "What do you feel? And are you sure you could Love someone like this?" To which I responded, "I see Love. And yes, I could Love someone like this." We flashed back out of Lindsey's room, and into the room from earlier. I struggled to keep my bearings and my spirit returned to my earthly body.

When I spoke with Bryan about it, he discussed with me his thoughts on the symbolism in the 3 scars. He thought that there was much for me to meditate upon with regards to the symbols in "The Stations of the Cross." Upon hearing my story, he felt immediately impressed to discuss the three falls that Jesus made while carrying his cross, and the symbolism in each one. While there is much to be gleaned, I feel strongly that Bryan has offered great truth upon the vision. While I did understand the scars to be figurative and not literal on Lindsey's back, I thought they represented her pain that she has been through in her life with previous relationships. Bryan's assessment takes it several steps further to define it as the marking on a soul in a manner similar to the marking of Christ's soul. He felt that the marking could be symbolic to someone who is walking in Jesus' shoes and has suffered, hurt, and has carried pains and burdens with them during their time on Earth.

The analysis of the scars goes even deeper once the images and descriptions have been studied more in depth. I have to agree that the scars most definitely held greater meaning in the direction where Bryan felt led to

Gravity Calling

interpret. I am still amazed in the experience; the answer; the emotion; the lesson; the Love. Regardless of the identity of Lindsey being the subject of the experience, I know the greater lesson is in the construct and the concept of Love. As I am learning to feel again, it was important that the angels help me quickly grow in understanding spiritual Love. I am sure the heavenly lessons came with heightened frequency and amplitude due to how the rate in my earthly journey has increased. While I should emphasize that again, the lesson was on "Love," that in no way, shape, or form should be seen as an absolute with Lindsey – only the concept of the potential, and the spiritual understanding of the weight her soul has born throughout her time here on Earth.

...

The epiphany came in the recognition of the Mark of III upon Lindsey's back. It was the one aspect of the experience that left me without resolve. Though Bryan offered his guidance when I discussed the vision the following day with him, I almost dismissed his guidance because I still did not find enough resolve in his interpretation. But as I drove home, I realized that everything Bryan had said was again correct (as it always is) AND there was one more important concept that glued it all together. That concept was to be found in my pain. For during the first time I was going to meet Lindsey, I experienced a letdown of indescribable proportions to my soul when I received the text that said she wasn't feeling well that morning and would not make it to church. It introduced every form of doubt I could have, but I prayed for strength and tried to find resolve. Simple text messages and quotes on social net-

Mark of III

works were enough to become lost in hope once again. But the second time she did not show up – and this time with no explanation – my soul was on the verge of nuclear meltdown.

It was the single greatest explosion of emotions I had experienced since my divorce. And from the outside, it should have not held that much effect. I recognized this fact. I had dated before and had experienced the ups and downs after my divorce. But this time was different. This time my soul was experiencing its first moments of hope and subsequent disappointment. It was a virgin to these feelings. I did not quite know how to experience spiritual disappointment – but this was one of the lessons to be learned. As I pondered the events and reflected back on my experiences in the heavens, God helped me see on that ride home from Chattanooga that the three marks upon Lindsey's back indicated three separate trials for me. They alluded to Bryan's interpretation, but were intended to be experienced by me. These were the three tests I would have to endure to learn to find Love again. The second mark was the longest, indicating it would be the defining moment – the moment I would be tested the greatest and experience the biggest amount of emotional strife. And to this day, that second letdown of my soul was the greatest test of my soul I have ever experienced. It was also the turning point – the point where I would define that I was ready for this step in my spiritual life. The "Stations of the Cross" would be the definition of these three steps on my journey as I carried the weight of the cross upon my back in the final days of my spiritual transition from child to young adult. It was the final time of understanding how my earthly and spiritual walk coincided with each other, and how to handle the extremity of feelings bound by Love. For if Love is the bookend to this portion of the journey – the beginning and the end, my soul would have to be primed to deem it worthy to carry the burden of the earthly struggles with faith as its foundation. But that portion would be better understood in the weeks to follow. For now, one last test remained. And the third test would prove to merge every concept I once had of the spiritual and earthly divide into one, bound only by which set of eyes are used in interpretation of the world around us.

Smiled For An Hour

The third test came on the Thursday evening heading into the Sunday we were to see each other again for the first time (which would be our third attempt at meeting up). The week began with the lingering question of how the second test would end. I had already found peace within the signs of the dove and the hawk and found comfort in my King for everything that he had shown me about Lindsey. For the mind, though, the sickening feeling of not even having any response to her absence was still uncomfortably lingering. But, that all changed Sunday evening when Lindsey reached out to me apologizing for missing our second meeting. While something so simple wouldn't seem to hold within it the significance I found, to see the world through the eyes of the other binds the mind to another level of understanding, peace, and resolve. In her answer, I saw reassurance from God in everything that He was telling me. And though I hate "games" when it comes to messaging back someone, in this moment I knew space said more than action. I waited until Monday to text her back. The words I chose to use would set our level of engagement for the week.

Late Monday evening, I replied to her, "No worries. I have waited three and a half years to say 'Good to see you again' so I think I can waiting a little longer. Though I'd hate to think we swung and missed three times at church of all places...:)" That text sent off a flurry of texts back and forth between us. It was the first time we had been engaged in fluid conversation since that night three and a half years ago. She asked if it had really been that long. I told her that it indeed had. In playful text-speak, I suggested bonus-points if she remembered where. She replied with two places – one that was actually where we met. She knew, but didn't want to let on completely. It was the first time I was witnessing souls speak directly to each other – playfully hiding beneath the context and phrasings of the words sent back and forth to each other. From this point of view, it was beautiful. I must've smiled for an hour straight during that conversation

As she danced around directly answering the question of where we first met, I let her know that I knew by telling her that she was sitting at the corner table in the specific restaurant, sitting on the left having dinner. Though she put up playful defenses questioning how I would remember, my soul gracefully waltzed around her questions telling her just enough to let her know I remembered. It was a dance of words and conversation that left each of our souls with reassurance that what happened the first night we met was real, was true. In the subsequent evenings, the conversations stretched for hours in fluidity. I wish I could have just picked up the phone and talked to her, but I knew that crossing that line could be too aggressive with her heart. Sometimes there is something special about distance, though for me it was more like agony-with-a-smile, where I knew it was what was needed in the midst of her rebuilding her life.

As our conversations began to become less of a playful dance of words and more of a direct communication between two souls, an unfortunate chain of events that occurred from early Thursday morning through Friday afternoon became a personal testament of faith – proof of my strength in God and demonstration of my recognition of His words, His guidance. This was the third test – a final demonstration of my soul's ability to endure the toughest tests set before me on my journey into the rising sun. Though it would appear it all would begin with a series of ill-timed events and texts Thursday evening, the truth is that it began early Thursday morning with a visit from a man in rose-colored glasses.

Rose-Colored Glasses

The heavens are a beautiful place. But in understanding that the heavens are a series of locations, it is important to understand that the destination between here and the holiest of holy locations can carry negative potential. In fact, as a soul becomes more aware of its call to origin, and in that, a call to perfection, the negative forces literally try to intervene and derail the soul's course. There are places these negative forces have limited dominion, though they cannot hurt you. For God created All That Is, and these negative energies should be best seen as those who identify with ego, stalled on their journey to Love and perfection. These are children of God who are lost. It is how Lucifer came to be. It is how "demons" are perceived to exist. Only through the spirit can one begin to understand that these demons are just lost souls – souls themselves searching for a way home. They are not "evil" or to be feared. They should best be seen only as speed bumps along the way of the journey who can do nothing but attempt to pull the soul's vibratory level down to theirs along the road of faith. But faith always wins. Faith will always prevail.

During the early morning hours on Thursday, I experienced a series of spiritual encounters that set the tone for the next thirty-six hours of my life. Each time I closed my eyes and removed that last sense from my mind, my spirit travelled to the heavens. During my first experience of the evening, I came face-to-face with a being that exuded all-things-negative – one whom I would come to realize is the commanding General of Anxiety's army. Some could argue it was Lucifer himself. This was a final test of my faith. To each person, I am sure this entity appears in ways that their spirit is able to recognize. To mine, he appears as another person – but much different in presentation than angelic beings. He is often wearing a blue suit – a suit that is flashy with a touch of sheen. It is clear that he is concerned about image and wants to portray himself as flashy to catch the eyes of those around him. Perhaps it could be thought of in a way similar to a flashy 1970's suit – wider collar, sharper edges, more pizazz. He also generally appears with slicked back hair and well-manicured facial hair. His build could best be thought of a lanky, but not meek. This time, he wore rose-colored glasses – round, for fashion and not necessity. But it is the filth, the disgusting nastiness that permeates his being that allows the soul to recognize his presence. If God can best be spiritually felt through an all-consuming feeling of warmth and Love, this man would represent everything uncomfortable and disgusting in one feeling. He constantly pushes the spiritual equivalent of earthly temptations into view, trying to draw the spirit off course. His presence is not unfamiliar, though I would say he only seems to enter into my journey when the greatest testaments of faith are about to occur.

Rose-Colored Glasses

In the first experience of the morning where the man in rose-colored glasses appeared, he tempted me by sending an overtly-sexual female being into the room I was in. She was flirty, trying to seduce me with her presence. She tried to give me expensive luxury items – a gaudy fur coat in particular. As soon as I told the girl that I did not want the coat, the man snaked his way into the room and the girl left. And perhaps "snake" is an appropriate word because that is how he moves; his movements are like unto the way a snake moves in fluidity. As soon as he appeared, my soul writhed from the disgust and filth. He made a gesture with his hands and told me, "I don't think she is the one for you" implying Lindsey and my path with her. I immediately tried to exit the room as quickly as I could and call my soul to return to my body, ridding myself from his presence. It was an experience that would attempt to stain my soul, though I was able to find my way back to my earthly body in breath.

But that experience was just the start of events to come. Each time I closed my eyes trying to find a more loving location in the heavens, I found myself in another haunting place where good and evil were divided. There were places of safety – inside of certain houses, but outside of the houses it seemed that negative energy had equal dominion. When leaving one house, I tried to drive to my next destination. I was warned to take roads where I would not be seen. In my periphery, I could see flashing lights and police officers arresting good souls that were wandering outside of the houses. I eventually had to go through a roadblock where I was asked to get out of my vehicle. I wasn't fearful, but I knew this was something that I was supposed to experience so I allowed it to happen. I was eventually taken to a prison to watch how lost souls suffer. I wasn't arrested per se, but I was told I must witness how these souls live. I witnessed T-bars in the rafters of the prison that the souls clung to in an inverted fashion – like bats in a cave. They were all stacked upon each other in the tightest of spaces. This is how they slept. The souls were filthy and disgusting, though they seemed overtly sexual with each other. I eventually called my soul to leave the place and returned to my earthly body.

    At this point, I decided to just try to sleep, but my body was already in an optimal "unlocked" position for journeying into the heavens, so as I closed my eyes again, I found myself sitting in a room of other beings listening to an instructor. I couldn't discern what he was saying, so I sat there just trying to observe how everyone in the room was reacting to his words. It seemed as if everyone was coupling off with another person of their choice. As I sat there, the girl sitting next to me nudged me to get my attention. I looked at her – she was very pretty and exuded sexuality, but not an object of loving warmth that other angelic bodies radiate. It was at this point I realized I was in another place where my soul was being tested. As I looked at her, she looked at me longingly, but playfully. She was wearing a revealing, deep-cut piece of draped cloth that barely covered her breasts. She had a very beautiful body. Her words to me were direct, straight to the point. She leaned over and told me aloud, "I'll have sex with you." Completely confused as to what was happening and the directness of her words, I tried to play it off with uncomfortable comedy. I just said, "You will? Awesome." and high-fived her. But her hand didn't let go. She held on. We sat there hand-in-hand as my mind tried to understand the moment.

Sex in the heavens is an interesting subject in and of itself, but it should be seen more as a spiritual union between two angelic beings destined to be. Sex in a casual sense could be best viewed as lost souls fighting through temptations. In both cases, sex is a very important part of spirituality. But understanding the significance and reason in sex is what makes it that much more special when a soul find's its soul-mate. As the spirit grows stronger, it becomes more apparent that sex is a spiritual union – destined to happen with two souls in monogamy. So, to be tempted by another with sex on a spiritual journey is often a test of the strength of the soul. This is what was occurring in this moment with me and is a typical temptation when negative energies are present – though this should not cause misinterpretation of sex as a negative act. I honestly believe it should be experienced at every available moment with the one you Love. Love is intended to be experienced on Earth through passion raging ferociously between two souls – the skin-to-skin igniting of the flesh to the touch, bound by a spiritual Love of even greater magnitude.

Shortly after we high-fived, all of the couples cleared out of the large room and we were left sitting in an empty room still holding hands. It was now apparent we had been sitting on a bed, and no longer was anyone around to distract from the situation. My casual comedy in the moment was no longer going to withstand her intentions. She immediately jumped into my arms and began trying to kiss me. I was still trying to digest what was going on because I knew that my heavenly walk would not have this type of situation happen without a purpose. As she tried to kiss me, I pulled back. I attempted to find a stalling tactic – again falling short of what was needed in that moment. I said, "Don't we need to go somewhere?" She just smiled and said, "No. I want it right here." She wrapped her legs around me and pulled me on top of her. Her shirt slid down around her sides revealing her breasts and stomach. She pulled me into kiss her more. I backed off of her and stood up. I told her, "Listen. I need you to know that I can't do this. I really like a girl whom you know and I cannot do anything that would hurt her." She looked at me both broken-hearted and confused, then ran off into the darkness around us.

    I sat on the bed mulling over the events that had taken place. I felt guilty for even allowing it to progress to the point where I had to break her heart, but at the same time I knew there was nothing I could do to prevent it because I had not rationalized the spiritual test quickly enough. My heart was heavy. As I sat there, the girl came back in and sat down beside me. This time she was larger in size, which helped me understand that she was an angel in disguise. She sat down next to me holding her knees in her arms – her bare feet fidgeting with each other in those moments. She asked, "So you really like her?" I said I did. She continued asking me about why I stopped being intimate with her. She asked why I would not be intimate when the girl I liked wasn't even around. She didn't leave me any room to answer between her questions, as they seemed more like a stream-of-consciousness thought process. When she paused, I told her, "Because some things are worth waiting for – and she is worth the wait."

It was at that point the girl began to reveal her true identity, stripping away the disguise she wore. She was indeed an angelic being sent to test my spirit. She asked me a couple of questions revealing that she knew the girl's identity, but didn't want to ask me directly; she wanted to hear my answers. After a series of questions, she eventually said, "Can I ask – is she named Lindsey?" I nodded. She said, "That is who I thought it was. She is dating someone else – just so you know." She also imparted an image to me of a guy with a goofy hairstyle by any standard. The angelic being turned to leave. It was as if the last thing she told me about the guy was a last-ditch effort to test me again, but without any effort put into the empty words. I told her, "That doesn't matter to me. She is worth waiting for, but please don't tell her. Please don't let her know you know about me. I want it to work, but she can't know about my feelings yet. I don't want to scare her off." The angel vanished into the distance. My spirit returned to my earthly body.

Was the angel a force of good or of negative potential? I don't know. Was the angel sent to test my faith, or add doubt? Again, I don't know. Was her telling me about Lindsey dating someone a truth or a lie, a way to add doubt or a way to test faith? Was the image of the guy to give me confidence in my own appearance to her, or to introduce doubt? Again I don't know. Perhaps it is all of the above – for the only thing that could possibly have been introduced to me was "fear" – and that part of my walk is unwavering. All I know is that the series of events that happened that evening were quite possibly one of the most stressful series of events I have encountered.

Spiritual tests are different than physical tests – they are extremely hard to put into words. But if I could try to sum it up, I would say that the observance of the actions of one's own spirit doesn't come with control or rationality – it is an observance in purity. earthly minds rationalize right or wrong, good or bad – and can help guide decisions when they need to occur. The soul acts in pureness of heart, without the rationality of the mind. The soul will act based on its level of purity, knowledge, and strength alone. Sometimes it can be disappointing to observe and experience, for the mind can rationalize the experience and help the soul grow, but acting in a way that is not as pure as the mind would like to demonstrate is disheartening. In this experience, I was proud to have successfully endured the tests, but I felt drained. After an evening of spiritual tests, my soul felt absent of energy and exuberance. And, as it would turn out, that feeling of my soul being drained was just the start of the manifestation of those spiritual experiences into the earthly walk heading into the day.

Puppeteer

To see the world as souls bound within the confines of the body and earthly influences is to understand the world on another level. Souls and the experiences witnessed in the heavens manifest in every day life. It becomes easier to sense goodness, and negative energies. In the periphery, the mind registers manifestations of the spiritual. Some people see auras. Some people see halos. Some people see angels. In whatever way the soul senses the spiritual presence in everything around us, the intricacies and details become easier to view as spiritual growth progresses – and to each, it will manifest in different ways. It is in everything unseen through which the soul moves in harmony with the body. For lost souls, it is much easier for negativity to influence their lives than those strong in faith. Maybe it appears as a desire to say something negative about another. Perhaps it is an action that didn't serve to help anyone, and instead introduces negativity or an obstacle into a situation. These are the actions that are set into motion by those wearing rose-colored glasses, acting as mystery puppeteers to the souls that are easily influenced, even though the puppets are blind to their actions being influenced due to their attachment to their own ego.

Gravity Calling

The events of my most recent spiritual encounter would play into my earthly life throughout the following Thursday and Friday morning. This was quite possibly the first time I had such a vivid understanding of how these energies puppeteer the easily-influenced, though I had been long aware of the influence most of my earthly life. By witnessing the events so closely together in spirit and earthly body, clarity was introduced into my understanding – for clarity is only further revealed through earthly experience. As I have emphasized before, the spirit appears in three forms: through everything around us, through another person, and directly through spiritual experiences. So for a soul to grow, it must also endure the circumstances of spiritual experiences in earthly form as a testament to spiritual growth.

On Thursday evening, Lindsey and I had begun our nightly conversation when she began to open up about her day. She had experienced what I can only imagine to be one of the most discouraging days a person can have at her job and maintain employment. As she began pouring out her heart to me over text, I had a knock at my door. This was the first time she had allowed herself to open up to me, and I knew in her words there was a delicacy in her actions – one that would require a delicate and timely response. I had just sent the last reply and knew that she would be sending her reply shortly, but the knock at my door took precedence in those moments. I knew my neighbor occasionally would stop by to borrow a movie or return one he had borrowed a few nights prior. It was typically very easy to dismiss him if I was busy.

Puppeteer

He was generally very short in his visits. But this time would prove to be different.

My neighbor came into my condo to return the movie he had borrowed a few days prior and saw that I was busy checking my phone and writing my book. In the recent weeks, it had become increasingly obvious that he was struggling with understanding his spiritual body, but as an atheist, he rejected religion in favor of science. During my ego-driven days, we were the best of friends. But over the course of my journey we had fallen apart, though it was a necessary step to move forward with my life. My soul could tell he was becoming curious about the changes in my life, even though I had never told him anything about my spiritual rebirth. His mind would not allow him to ask the questions when he did drop by. This made for some very awkward situations where he would knock on my door, come in and just stand a few feet inside my doorway without any questions, without words in reply to mine. The few subjects he would ramble about were masked attempts to prod into what direction my life had taken and why I was so peaceful, but I never allowed my answers to reveal anything he didn't ask directly. The last he really knew me, I was encumbered by darkness flailing about, looking for anything I could hold onto to help me climb out. But now I treated his indirect questions like a spiritual game of cat-and-mouse until he asked directly. It was something I had come to expect periodically in his presence. And this time would appear no different on the surface.

Gravity Calling

So on the Thursday evening he entered into my condo, I recognized this could be another one of those conversations. But as he stood in my condo, just a few feet inside of the door, I became aware it was so much more than just my assumption of his mind seeking reason. This was a moment of spiritual puppetry. At this point along my journey I had become aware that the soul is like a porous sponge before it gains spiritual strength. It drinks of all the influences around it – good or negative – both while it is incubating and even in its time of rebirth as a child. It is in the time prior to rebirth that people experience "gut feelings" and act in response. These are the actions the spiritual puppeteers invoke on the soul. They are a set of strings that connect the soul to a commanding force, evoking the ego to react to its call. And as much as I do not want my words to be mistaken or taken out of context, the only way I could phrase what I was witnessing was to parallel my neighbor as the puppet and the man in rose-colored glasses as the puppeteer. It was a timing that could only have happened to disrupt and interfere in a moment of great importance in my life.

It took nearly thirty minutes for my neighbor to leave. Every time I would check my phone I would begin to type a response to Lindsey's question, he would intentionally pull my attention away. It was possibly the most frustrating half hour I have ever experienced because I witnessed the puppeteering in action before me. I knew it wasn't my neighbor as a person as much as he was just blindly serving as a vessel for the negative energy to permeate the importance of the moment. There

Puppeteer

even came a time when I told him he needed to just hang on and give me some time to reply back to an important text. But as I read Lindsey's text, I realized everything she was telling me in the conversation required a delicate response – a response wherein I could allow my spirit to speak to hers, unencumbered by the negative energy trying to act upon me at that point in time. Try as I may to write the best response I could, my neighbor would continue to randomly talk and pull my attention away. I eventually set my phone down and decided it was best to figure out how to resolve his questions.

After thirty agonizing minutes placed upon my soul, he finally strolled out. I could not tell you even more than a sentence or two of what he was talking about. It all seemed like random gibberish that held no glue – and likely it was just that. For a puppet can only act out the pulls and tugs from within, however broken in context they may seem. When I returned to Lindsey's text, I replied back as quickly as I could as my soul sought to save the moment, though I already knew the gap in time coupled with her soul's delicacy had caused anxiety and placed doubt upon her decision to open up to me. Her last text to me during those agonizing thirty minutes was an apology for opening up to me with two emoticons of a crying face. There would be no more responses from her, even in the wake of my reply. My soul was crushed. It wasn't as if I had ignored her, or even unconsciously kept her at bay. It wasn't even a moment where something of precedence came crashing down around me. Instead, my soul went to war with the man in rose-colored glasses. He attacked me in the form of

Gravity Calling

a Trojan horse entering into my house – a knock on my door that I answered and allowed into the walls of my home.

It was the first time I was fully spiritually aware in the active moment how the influences of the spiritual world work in the physical world. We are all taught to believe that angels are there to guide us, to help us in moments of need. They offer divine intervention in situations of importance, often arriving in the forms of strangers. But it is rarely considered that the very people closest to us will serve as a spiritual vessel between the heavens and earthly worlds. And even if a person chooses to accept that a person can be a harbinger of hope and divine intervention from angels, it is even a tougher thought to realize those same people can serve as the puppets for the man in rose-colored glasses. No one wants to think of the potential of evil, for it introduces fear and doubt in the unknown. And perhaps it even makes a person feel guilty to consider a close friend influenced by such a negative force. Blind naiveté provides a false sense of comfort and hope where its fallacy is only revealed once a soul begins to see every human form as housing a soul, able to be influenced and puppeteered by the angels and even the man in rose-colored glasses. It is through the eyes of the soul that the influences become apparent and discernible. But until the eyes of the soul are able to see unobscured from ego's influence, the ability to discern what force is commanding the puppet will have to remain a gut feeling and a mental rationale on the odds – a blind naiveté to the reality of the situation at hand.

Fear of Falling

A spiritual war began the day I allowed the Trojan horse into the walls of my home. To this point, I had been physically tested, spiritually tested, and was now experiencing the manifestations of the spiritual tests into the physical world. It was a lesson in learning how to blend my understandings of both worlds into one. While the man in rose-colored glasses may have thought he won his surprise battle by injecting a higher dose of anxiety into me than I had ever experienced before, it would prove to be a futile attempt at winning the war. If anything, it opened my spiritual eyes even more than they were prior to his attempt to dismantle my soul.

In the moments following my reply text to Lindsey my very being was soaked in anxiety. At that point, my mind had embarked on a roller coaster of fear – fear that somehow, within those thirty minutes of space between text messages, a doubt was introduced into her mind that would forever alter the course of what I believed to be the destination. I felt my faith waiver in the midst of Anxiety's last stand. The emotions I was experiencing were what I could only compare to how a child first starts experiencing the rush of emotions in puberty. I struggled to gain control of my thoughts as they pranced rampantly around my mind. After continuing to check my phone

Gravity Calling

for a response over the next couple of hours, I eventually gave up. Disheartened, I headed to bed to pray and find rest. My spirit was exhausted.

As I lay in bed, I began to think of ways to let her soul know that I was still there, despite the doubt that could have crept into her mind. And perhaps, the doubt was stronger in my mind than hers. It is entirely possible that I created a situation based on my own fear that was introduced to me in that situation. I reflected on where the fear was rooted, why it was rooted, if there was actually truth to support the fear at all. I eventually rationalized that the circumstance I found myself in was the only circumstance that God intended for me. He could just as easily have swayed my neighbor to not come over if I wasn't going to overcome the obstacle set before me and grow into a stronger person. I realized it was a test of faith – and a test of recovery. Would I flail about seeking to recover and potentially cause more damage, or would I realize that I just needed to find my spiritual center and act as called upon? At this point, everything that God had shown me about Lindsey should have already offered me more than enough resolve in knowing the eventual destination, but anxiety introduced fear.

I concentrated on centering myself. I attempted to meditate, though it took a while for me to find calm within the storm. But as I did, in the calm of my mind, I realized that I was granted a great opportunity. I ended my meditation and communed with God in prayer. It was more of a rambling of thoughts than a prayer seeking answers. After my prayer, I allowed my mind to wonder. I composed countless text messages I planned to send the following day that were crafty, but said what my soul needed to say. All fell short in my intention. I eventually decided that I needed a grander demonstration of my soul. While we still had yet to see each other still, I had to search within to find a careful line of action. I eventually arrived at chocolate. Every woman lights up to chocolate – though it would be in the action of my efforts that my soul would find a voice without my physical name attached.

There is a local chocolate company down the road from my condo that offers great gift boxes with handmade chocolate. The boxes look more like handmade gift boxes than anything romantic in gesture (which I wanted to avoid for obvious reasons), so I thought it would be perfect. I decided that I would send a box to her and each of her coworkers at her office without my name attached. If nothing else, it would serve as a nice surprise to all of them, and hopefully bring some happiness to their day. I composed a thoughtful text message that I planned to send later the following afternoon to Lindsey asking if they enjoyed the chocolate. I found peace in my intended action, though I had a lot of trouble sleeping.

As I lay in bed awake, I realized that it was the first time in my life I had a fear of falling asleep. My soul was exhausted from the last several nights of tests and I did not want to experience seeing the man in the rose-colored glasses again. After all, I had just witnessed him puppeteering in my home earlier in the evening. While I knew there was nothing he could do to me in the heavens, it still gave me a feeling of filth and discom-

Gravity Calling

fort when I thought about his presence. I rolled over and texted Bryan – who I knew was asleep at that time. We had not talked in over a week, so he was not aware of any of my recent experiences in the heavens or much of my situation with Lindsey. Our paths had diverged somewhat as we each embarked on the personal parts of our spiritual journeys. My text to him was concise. I mentioned that it was the first time I was afraid of falling asleep after seeing the man in rose-colored glasses again. I mentioned nothing of Lindsey, the chocolate, or anything similar. I didn't expect a response so I rolled back over and prayed some more. I asked God for guidance that my gesture would be the right thing. I had a history of doing "too much" and I didn't want to fall victim to that past habit. I just needed somehow a vote of reassurance. At 4 a.m. – approximately three hours after I had texted Bryan, I was awakened by a text message. It was from Bryan. The text read:

...

"You can't truly appreciate the sweet until you've truly experienced the bitter."

...

I had to reread the text I sent him to make sure I said nothing about chocolate or Lindsey. I could not believe the words I was reading. God found a way to answer my prayer through Bryan. I replied back letting him know how divinely inspired his words were. I just received a smiley face in return. Even at a later point, when I asked him about why he phrased his message to me in the way he did, he told me he awoke

Fear of Falling

from a vision, saw my text message, and knew those were the words I needed to hear. These were words instructed for him to share with me, not architected by his own mind. So as I lay awake at 4 a.m., I now realized my actions were just – and that the words of Bryan's text alluding to chocolate were the voice of God – words I needed to hear to start my day. I went ahead and began my morning hours earlier than usual. I took a lot of time to just meditate and thank God before I went by the chocolate store before work. But as it turns out, this was only the beginning.

Blushing Berry

Apparently, the war that began with the Trojan horse was still raging. The General of Anxiety's army decided it would pull out all of the stops as I sought to respond in the victorious way that God intended. The war began at 730 a.m., just a few minutes before I planned to leave my house to go by the chocolate store. I also had an appointment at 8 a.m. that I could not miss and a 9 a.m. meeting that I was leading at my office. Just to make sure I knew what time the store opened, I checked their website for hours of operation. But the man in rose-colored glasses delivered his first shot of the morning to me in that moment. Apparently they are closed on Fridays...and Fridays only. I didn't see that one coming.

I immediately began to flail, looking for any other chocolate stores that were local and could offer similar packaging. But for the handful of stores I found, each one only offered the cliché heart shaped or romance-inspired gift boxes – or had closed in the wake of poor business. None of these would do. I knew that I needed the chocolate to arrive first thing in the morning and I felt that it was extremely important that it was delivered no later than 11 a.m. at the latest (though I would not come to find out why I felt so strongly about the time or arrival until days later). This was no longer just a spiritual gesture from my soul to hers. It had become a testament in my ability to respond to God's words and remain unswayed by the man in rose-colored glasses. It turns out the only other store I found in the Nashville area opened at 10 a.m., and would require a days notice for any order or delivery. I was already facing an uphill battle and it wasn't even 8 a.m. Finally, I ran across one last chocolate store mentioned in a local magazine – no website, no location. It received rave reviews in the magazine for a private event and, from the best I could tell, it could potentially offer everything I was looking for.

I left the house content with finding this store after my appointment. As I drove to my appointment, construction caused a two-mile drive to turn into thirty minutes. I arrived late, was delayed in getting started and left the location with merely ten minutes to drive fifteen miles to reach my meeting at the office at 9 a.m. As I drove, my gas light came on. I stopped to get a couple of gallons of gas where the pump took nearly five minutes to pump three gallons. It was clear that Anxiety was going to do its best in a fight with me that morning. But I continued undeterred, holding strong in my faith that these speed bumps were just put in place so that I could show my demonstration of faith and acknowledgement of His response to my prayer the previous night. I arrived at my meeting fifteen minutes late, led a brief strategy session, and then got back in my Jeep to find the location of the chocolate store. It was 9:30 a.m. and I still had no idea where I was driving. It was blind faith.

Blushing Berry

As I sat in my Jeep, I was able to find an address to the location and their hours of operation on my phone. It opened at 10 a.m. and was somewhere between thirty and forty-five minutes away from my office. I had to guess a range of drive-times because every GPS app and map in existence could not pinpoint the address. Apparently, the address was so new that satellite maps had not been updated yet. I set forth driving in the general direction of the location, unsure of my destination. I called, but only received a voicemail since the store was not yet opened. As I drove, I searched for other businesses with the same street address. I eventually ran across one – and only one. It was a nail salon.

I should have expected what was about to occur, but I held onto hope that this would be a moment of clarity for my destination. But as the phone rang and a voice rang out, I found myself speaking to a lady who barely spoke any English and did not know how to describe where they were located. She handed the phone to her husband who was extremely kind. I could tell that he had a good soul just by the way he tried to help me. He eventually was able to describe in much less broken English the general location of where they were. I was given surrounding street names and landmarks, though it was a city I had never been to. We ended our conversation, and I felt happy – content that I had found resolve.

As I headed in that direction, I spent the next 30 minutes figuring out who I knew that could ride with me and serve as a delivery person. I left a lot of messages, but headed to the store without resolve in having anyone definite to help me. At this point my time was running short and I knew I would have to deliver the chocolate, but by no means could I do it in person. That would defeat the anonymous gesture. Eventually after a few wrong turns and warding off Anxiety, I arrived at Blushing Berry at 9:59 a.m. The store opened at 10 a.m., so I waited for them to unlock the door...they never did. At 10:10 a.m. I walked up to the door noticing there were two employees inside when one of them took notice of me and came to unlock the door, apologetic for forgetting. As it turned out, this would be the very first day they were opened for business in a storefront, and I was their very first customer...ever. Everything else had been private events or through word-of-mouth.

    The mother and daughter owners were beautiful souls. It was clear that the journey to Blushing Berry was another important part of my journey so I could witness the divine script in play. How else could the events of the day line up so precisely? The exact day that I was sent on a mission to deliver chocolate and bring happiness to another, was the exact day that Blushing Berry would open its doors for the first time. It was the only day of the week that the other chocolate store was closed. I have to believe that the experience was intended for the owners of the store as well. I had an open budget and only asked that they create something perfect for Lindsey and her three nurse colleagues. I wanted four of everything in the basket. For the owners of Blushing Berry, it was a perfect business opportunity and a moment of inspiration of opening their doors for the first time. For me it was an answered prayer.

Blushing Berry

They went on to make a beautiful basket of handmade chocolates and baked goods that said everything my soul wanted to express. It was every word I could hope to say crafted in a way that only the souls at Blushing Berry could do. Wrapped up in the perfect creation they made, and in witness to the divine alignment of Blushing Berry opening its doors on the very day when I was on a mission to answer God's call, I witnessed the art of life; the art of seeing past each person's own strengths and weaknesses, fear and doubts, and seeing each person at their core, in a way they are intended to play a part in our lives at a divine time. It is in the art of life that souls find the right way to help other souls communicate in everything unsaid. Life is much more beautiful when seen from this viewpoint, and I hoped Lindsey's soul would see it as such as well.

I left the store. On my way toward her work, I finally was able to get in contact with a friend who was able to ride along with me to deliver the basket. Along the way my gas light came on again. I stopped to get gas where the pump continued to fail to connect to its payment processing company upon me swiping my card. I sat there for several minutes as it was "Authorizing." This was clearly another attempt by the man in rose-colored glasses to introduce anxiety into my life. Eventually the pump authorized, but pumped gas at a rate as slow as the pump I found earlier in the morning. Time was ticking away. Eventually I became satisfied I had enough gas for the journey and put the pump back in place. As I was about to drive away, I watched the pump reset and display, "Please Pay

Gravity Calling

Inside." I was thoroughly confused. I had swiped my card and the pump eventually turned on – something that doesn't happen if payment is refused. I went inside and waited in a long line where it was eventually explained that the pump was manually turned on because they were having connection problems. They processed my card and I drove away. Had I not seen that one small line of text on the pump that told me to pay inside when I was ready to pull away, I would undoubtedly have had one of the three cops in the parking lot (and who were standing inside by the cashier) chase after me for stealing gas. But I survived that test. The next fifteen miles of the journey consisted of traffic backed up behind construction vehicles and tractors on the road. I can say that I honestly spent the next twenty minutes of drive time driving twenty miles under the speed limit. My mental delivery-time cutoff was nearing and I was nowhere near her place of work.

I eventually made it through the construction and picked up my friend. He was wrapping up business at his house, so I experienced more delay before he made it out to my Jeep. When he finally made it out to my Jeep and his eyes saw the basket, I of course had to hear the "what are you thinking?!" conversation about my actions. On the surface level, I would have agreed – and I honestly expected to hear it from a friend. But this was a spiritual journey, though I listened as my friend spoke. He told me that he supported me regardless and that he hoped I knew what I was doing, but that he thought it was a terrible idea. If the man in rose-colored glasses wanted to make one last stand, this was his greatest attempt, for words have the power to affect the soul more greatly than through actions alone. But I was prepared. I drove in confidence to my destination. As we chatted, I told my friend that it was something I was supposed to do and that I appreciated his advice, but I was extremely confident in my walk. Eventually I noticed the tug on his soul in another direction – this time from an angelic puppeteer in the midst of conversation. It was a moment that would have been easy to miss earlier in my all-or-nothing perception of good and negative influences, for it was much more subtle in delivery than I would have expected.

As we chatted, he struggled to understand the rationale in my gesture. He asked me why I was sending the basket anonymously and why I was sending it to all of her close coworkers as well. I explained they had all experienced a tough time at their work, but that there was a careful safety in the way I was delivering my sentiments to her – something that said everything I needed to say without it coming off as too powerful for one person. He thought about it for a minute and responded with, "Well, I would just offer you this advice. If it is anonymous and she wants it to be from you, she will believe it was from you and eventually seek to find out. If she does not want it to be you yet – if it would scare her away – then she won't allow herself to think it was you…that is assuming you two have the type of connection the way you have described."

I thought about his words and acknowledged the divine message housed within. I debated on whether it was one last way to introduce doubt, but could see the great difference in his spiritual delivery. We arrived at the destination just a few minutes after 11 a.m. I drove to a discreet part of the parking lot behind the building while he went inside and delivered the basket. I wanted to make sure there was not a chance of my vehicle being seen. He came back and told me he dropped it off with a group of nurses who said they would take it right over to the intended recipients. I felt satisfied and warm in the moment. We drove off to grab lunch. No sooner as we had pulled out of the parking lot of Lindsey's work than I received a text. It was from Lindsey. She was apologizing for being a "terrible texter" and not responding last night. It was a playful text and well crafted with a smile at the end. And though I had still planned on sending a text later in the afternoon to mention the chocolate, I put that thought on pause to process the gravity of the moment. Without words, without any indication the delivery was from me – her soul knew in an instant and immediately responded in kind. And that was all I needed. I would not text her until the evening, leaving time for the conversation of our souls to resonate. And in my text, I would not mention the chocolate.

    Maybe it was in the proximity of our souls being near each other for the first time in three and a half years that sent a tremor deep within her soul, or possibly just in the energy my soul put into the effort alone. But whatever the true reason, it was a moment I realized that words were no longer required in my spiritual walk. The very action of my gesture spoke to her soul in a way that spiritual conversation only can. And in that, I found resolve. We met on a day that our souls collided, and I plan to continue that spiritual conversation in unspoken words for as long as we are bound. I never told her the delivery from Blushing Berry that day was from me – and though I will if she chooses to ask me, for now I have peace in knowing that she will one day discover it as she reads the words in this book. I came to learn in the following days that Lindsey's office closes at noon on Fridays and my impetus to have the delivery there before their day ended was even more spiritually driven than I was aware. For me I thought the timeline to make sure the basket was delivered before 11 a.m. was so it would be there for them to experience a morale booster for the remainder of the day. But as it turns out, it was a way to send a stamp of happiness into the weekend as the work week came to an end. That is just how the spirit works sometimes. We aren't always privy to the reason, but we must follow through with the response as we are led through His Will.

The Sunday following this third and final spiritual trial, Lindsey and I would see each other again for the first time. It was a time of "good to see you agains" and a time of spiritual rejoicing. She would have no idea of the battles I had faced before this day arrived. I would meet her kids for the first time and she would introduce me to her pastor following the service. During the service I watched as she tried to hold her nerves at bay, though they still managed to seep out through the cracks. It was beautiful. She was beautiful. I couldn't hold back my smiles. It was undeniably one of the greatest days of my life. The service was the second in a series entitled "Let Hope In" and the chosen song of worship during the service was "White Flag" – a song that could not have been more divinely architected to the script of my life. For just as Dance of Knight was a chapter that had been long written and titled before God's intervention through the dove and the hawk seven days prior, the chapter entitled White Flag Waiving had also been penned and titled the same day Dance of Knight was completed. Two back-to-back chapters I had written mirrored through His hand, held together seven days apart.

The first time Lindsey and I would see each other again in over three and a half years occurred in the house of God. It was a day of worship and a day of celebration. It was a day of His divine acknowledgement peppered in song, that two souls had found each other once again. This was the start of my Deuteronomy, the fifth act on my journey into the Promised Land. Somehow along the way, in the midst of the darkness, the North Star that Lindsey represented when she was so divinely placed into my life preceding my Genesis, shined brightly enough that I was able to take notice and find my way home. Anxiety had still not finished fighting its final battle, but in the weeks following I would be called to take a seven day journey to Haiti where God offered me every bit of guidance to help me learn to extinguish Anxiety's forces of un-resolve. It is where this book took its final form, and where the full understanding of the journey as five great acts fell into view. It became a place I watched a child die in the heavens and a young man be born.

Haiti

On a Wednesday evening in January of 2014, I was led to make a decision that became one of the next defining moments of my life. Nashville had recently fallen nature's victim to a nor'easter winter blast of cold air that had lingered for the past several weeks. Temperatures were an uncharacteristically cold 9 degrees Fahrenheit. While Nashville's weather is always in flux, it is rarely below freezing for more than a couple of days at a given time in winter. This time was different. This time the cold weather had outlived its welcome. I began to mull over when I should take a vacation from Nashville. A few days prior I had an experience in the heavens where an angel told me to leave Nashville for a while, but I was insistent I needed to stay because "there was something I still needed to do." In the conversation with the angel, I thought it could be another test about not allowing my course to be undeterred with Lindsey, but upon reflection I realized it was not a test, but rather a strongly encouraged directive. So as I sat on my couch thinking about when, where, and whether I should take a vacation, God spoke to me in the silence. I was told to buy a ticket to Haiti and to go for 7 days. I was to have no other plans other than to arrive with my backpack and whatever I might need over those 7 days. So I booked a flight and two days later, I stepped foot in Haiti – the first country I would ever visit outside of the United States or border country Mexico.

Haiti became a metaphorical journey to my spiritual and earthly walk, but it would take a day or two of wandering around the country to understand the purpose in the trip. Metaphorically, the days of wandering were no different that the beginning of my Genesis – and the rest of the trip would play out in similar metaphorical fashion. Arriving only with a backpack, my iPad to work on my book if needed, and ultralight camping paraphernalia, I hopped off the plane eager to see what was before me. But what I found is what I could only describe as a beautiful mess.

It began with discovering there was no way to exchange currency in the airport, followed immediately by discovering no one understood English...at all. Somehow I had imagined that English was universal enough to scrape by on some key words and hand gestures. Just a word of advice – it is not going to happen in Haiti. I quickly had to search the depths of my mind to blow off 15 years worth of dusting that rested on top of a few French classes I took during high school and college. These were enough to help me drudge by – but only on essentials. I chose to not use my mobile phone or internet during my trip. This was seven days I needed to experience as a stranger in a foreign land – tasked only by the directive from God. So I began wandering. I wandered in the wrong direction and eventually righted my ways. I searched for a bank eventually finding someone with enough broken English who

Haiti

was happy to take me to a bank....with his ten friends in tow behind him. I surprisingly made it to the bank where I was greeted by a man with a shotgun questioning why I had a horde of Haitians following me – but he spoke in French and I could not answer him. I walked in with three of the Haitians and eventually exchanged $100 – which is equivalent to 25% of the annual median income of the population in Haiti. The men that helped me expected payouts for getting me to the bank. So I obliged.

I left the bank, and was immediately surrounded by around fifteen people wanting to escort me around Haiti, but I told them I was walking. Everyone laughed at my answers – partly due to my broken French, partly due to the unforeseen absurdity to my answer. But I began hiking. I walked through a city that was filled with trash everywhere. If the trash wasn't burning, it was piled up with farm animals and the homeless sifting through the remains. I eventually found a group of Americans sitting on the back of a pickup truck waiting to go to their destination. I was excited someone spoke English, but discovered they were going to the opposite side of the country than where I intended to go. They were extremely puzzled that I was alone and backpacking in a country where I could not speak the language, had no plans, and had no one around to help prevent the occasional angry white-man hate I would come to experience. But I found safety in God. He had sent me on a journey where I had to have faith in His intended destination.

Gravity Calling

So I walked. I walked for hours until nightfall. The further I walked, the more I felt like I was near the end of nowhere with no destination in sight. All I wanted to find were two trees to throw my hammock between so I could rest and remove the backpack from my shoulders. But I neither found two trees, nor a place of rest. As it turns out, nearly every tree in inner Haiti has been cut down and harvested. Around nightfall I decided to seek a faster way out of town. The map I had used for my initial hike had a poor scale of distance. And where I thought I would be hiking for maybe ten miles to my first stopping point, as it would turn out, it was more like thirty or forty miles. So I hopped on the back of a moto and went for a ride.

The most thrilling, and simultaneously terrifying, thing I would come to learn about Haiti is the fact there are no driving laws. There is pavement that is about the width of two lanes, but if people want to drive three cars wide in the same direction, everyone else must react and pull off of the road or play chicken while blaring their horns to see who flinches first. And drivers of moto's (which are basically dirt-bikes) essentially drive wherever they please. In between semi-trucks, on the left side of the road, on the right side of the road, passing on the shoulder, passing on the center line – anything goes. Oh – and speed bumps are placed in random spots where traffic needs to slow down but are left unmarked. So as I hopped on the back of a moto – with no helmet of course – we sped off into the distance searching for my destination. Truthfully I planned on hopping off wherever I saw two trees.

Haiti

But we drove for another half hour with no trees in sight. The weight of the backpack was now crushing my shoulders while we drove. In the darkness the driver navigated pretty well. My flashlight on its lowest setting was brighter than his headlight and I debated on pulling it out to illuminate the road. There are no streetlights in Haiti. There is barely even electricity. But I trusted he knew what he was doing....that is until we hit a speed bump while going about forty miles an hour. While the entire moto caught air and both the driver and I left our seats for a brief moment, we each held on and managed to land in one piece without crashing. When we came to a stop immediately after that happened, the driver just looked at me and muttered something in French that I could only imagine were a slur of curse words in amusement of us surviving. Eventually I decided to find a hotel (which is basically someone's house converted for guests) and found some rest.

The next day I awoke and chatted with a Haitian that spoke English named Edward Craft. He was an artist and the brother to the woman who owned the hotel. He showed me some of his work placed around the hotel. On the surface, his art would first appear to be poorly proportioned paintings of people and bizarre situations. But as I studied the art, I realized everything he did had a purpose, had a meaning. I started to see all of the spiritual meanings in his art – the numerology in the number of items, the geometry it was based on, the reason in the proportions. Whether he intended the art to demonstrate those features or he was divinely inspired, I wasn't sure – and truthfully it didn't matter. I knew the hotel I found was purposed for me on my journey by God. The meeting with Edward Craft had spiritual purpose. When I commented on some of the things I observed in his art, his eyes lit up. I am pretty sure no one else had ever observed his intentions and he became extremely excited. He took me to a room filled with hundreds of paintings he had completed and showed me the symbolism in each of his favorite paintings. I listened as I heard God speak through this man to me. His words held purpose and meaning for my visit. If I had some way to return with the paintings, I would have purchased several, but I had no way to carry a painting while backpacking alone.

After chatting for an hour and listening to his suggestions on where I was planning on visiting while in Haiti, I set off in search of an orphanage I knew was in the area – the reason I chose this particular area as my first destination. However, as small as the village was I found myself in, no one seemed to know where the orphanage was. I even knew the French word, but it fell on deaf ears. Perhaps it was my accent that distorted the pronunciation of the word. Either way, I had to aimlessly wander to seek it out. Eventually I found my way through a neighborhood and found a walled off school yard in the general vicinity of where Edward told me the orphanage was. Perhaps Edward thought the school was the orphanage. But the school was a Christian ministry – a funded effort by a religious organization outside of Haiti. I went into the school yard and eventually met the man who ran the school. He spoke

Haiti

about as much English as I did French so it was a struggle to communicate both ways – but our souls found communion. I wanted to volunteer and help with anything they needed, but somewhere the translation didn't quite work out. Instead I was escorted around to each classroom to meet all of the children – about 200 in total.

It was an amazing moment. All of the children lit up when I walked into the room. It was evident they had not seen many foreigners (if any). They all told me they were so happy to see me and I would reply back to each classroom in my broken French. The children would do anything to touch my hand, to feel my spirit. It was a very spiritual experience in the midst of a broken country. As I was escorted around the school, the children followed. Children in each class left their classrooms to continue following me around my tour, all while reaching out just to touch my hands – high fives, holding hands, fist bumps. The method of touch didn't matter – just that there was touch at all. As I wrapped up meeting all of the children, I was fed lunch. It was a moment I was unprepared to experience because every resource in Haiti is so highly valued. But the leaders wanted to feed me, to welcome me in. I was humbled. At the end of lunch, we exchanged phone numbers and it has now become my mission to one day return with resources to help them continue their ministry. The school really only consisted of cement walls and shared plank desks. I didn't see any books, or any other resources to help in learning. Aside from one or two chalkboards for the ten or so classrooms I visited, that is all they really had – and a chapel. On

Gravity Calling

the outside of the chapel were several verses from Psalms painted in vibrant colors, that warmed my heart to see.

I left the school and continued onto my destination several hours away in Jacmel. I knew there were beaches in the area and therefore palm trees must exist. Never did I think I would have such a hard time finding trees for my hammock to camp. Nor did I expect to not be volunteering at the orphanage I assumed was the reason for my journey. I learned how to take the other death-defying forms of travel around the country: tap-taps, buses, and even crazier moto drivers. I took the journey through the mountains where I witnessed broken down trucks and broken down buses that couldn't complete the trip. And for every mid-sized pick-up truck, there were roughly fifteen people crammed into the back of each one. One truck had even caught fire and burned to a crisp. I saw another truck that had driven off the side of the embankment in moments that just preceded me passing by. To this day, I feel fortunate to have made it through alive – but this is a daily experience for people in Haiti, who take it in stride.

But as the end of my second day of wandering ended, I found a hotel about eleven miles outside of Jacmel run by an older Swiss man. It was called Hotel Kabic Beach Club and was the perfect setting for me to unwind – the perfect setting for me to be inspired and reflect on the previous two days…not to mention he took credit cards which was important since I had not seen another bank since exchanging my first $100 of spending money earlier. This location turned into my oasis in the midst of the chaotic surroundings of Haiti, and one I came to understand as purposed for me during my journey. It was where I would experience some of my most important ever communions with the angels in the heavens. It is where I would understand the purpose of the trip He called me to take. Most importantly, it is where I would understand the full picture of my journey – from Genesis to Deuteronomy; from the journey into the darkness of the setting sun, into the rising sun of the Promised Land. It was all about to make sense.

Best of Me

On the morning of the third day, I awoke to a breathtaking, cloudless day. The previous night I had also experienced a series of trips to the heavens that I would not fully understand for days to come, but the experiences always left me inspired. The weather was perfect – somewhere in the mid-80s most of the day. I began the day with a breakfast of fresh fruit, coffee, and an omelet at the outdoor restaurant on the premises. Shortly into breakfast, surrounded only by the sounds of nature around me, I realized part of the purpose of my trip was to write – to complete the chapters of this book that I had not yet had time to finish. Most of those chapters were lodged somewhere between "Return to Genesis" and "Defining Moments." Somehow in my writing, I had understood the beginning and end, but had to fill in the gaps of the spiritual journey that helped tell the story. Most chapters were half way completed with notes at the end, so I at least had somewhere to begin.

After breakfast I parked myself at a table outside and began to write. I was inspired. The setting and the experience of Haiti allowed me to chug through a chapter or two before lunch. At lunch I went to the beach and tried to get some sun in order to even out the ghastly farmer's tan I had accrued over the last two days. Maybe it is just a pet-peeve of mine, but I cannot go to a warm climate and return with only my face and arms finding sun. So I spent a few hours on the beach. While I was there listening to only the waves crashing on the shore, I found clarity in God's choice of Haiti for me. It was in the beautifully broken way that the culture survived. It was a country that did not want help – and did not need help. There was nothing outsiders could find to fix that wasn't already solved and mended in such a way that the locals found beautiful.

While the country is the poorest country in the Western Hemisphere, and I'd have to guess is one of the dirtiest, it seemed that their culture had a way of life that was embraced. The country may not have the standards and conveniences that first-world foreigners have come to take for granted, but it was not necessary. There was a harmony among the people; a song I heard throughout the country. It was in this recognition that I saw Haiti begin to parallel with the starting point of a persons life heading into Genesis...and then Exodus. I started to see the story of the first five books of the Bible revealed as a progression of steps and the importance in their meanings. And while this book was already founded on the concept of Genesis and Love, I didn't quite see the whole parallel to the first five books of the Bible until the giant sucker punch to my soul that I experienced as I lay on the beach. I recognized my wanderings during the first two days were like unto my personal wanderings on my spiritual journey. It is a comparison I can't put fairly into words, but a comparison my soul heard in song.

I returned from the beach and continued writing – this time understanding how my spiritual journey had evolved in the particular way it had. The more I wrote, the more clarity I gained. This was the moment of hindsight for me where everything I had experienced was revealed. In writing I found recognition of the place I found myself in – both literally and figuratively in the sand. It was a moment I knew that I was staring at the Promised Land – that I had blindly followed His Voice throughout my journey, guided by the North Star that He placed in my life preceding my Genesis. The only book I had originally found any comparison in when I began writing this book was in how my darkness was like Genesis – but now I found strength in seeing it all in hindsight – the first four acts I had completed and the fifth one that remained. And if the morning view of the blue sky, cloudless day was breath taking, this moment of clarity was the gasp of air that filled my lungs with the oxygen to breathe, and my soul the oxygen needed to inflame the strength of the fire of my spirit inside once again.

The words flowed out faster than I could type. During four days of writing, I completed most of the final version of this book, barring a couple chapters at the very end. Every day I wrote, I knew God could see the words expressing my recognition of what He was telling me all along. When I realized the timing of each of the important steps I had written about along my journey (at the time they occurred), I wept. The hotel staff must have thought I had lost my mind if they witnessed my reactions throughout the days I wrote. I would weep, smile, and laugh as I reflected on each chapter I wrote. The weeping was my souls recognition of the abundance of God's Love. It wasn't crying. It was spiritual weeping – an entirely different concept in both experience and expression. By the end of the third day of writing, I had completed all of the chapters in between "Return to Genesis" and "And Then There Was Her." The beginning had already long been written, and the ending was in its final form.

It was every part of clarity wrapped up into a handful of chapters that I hoped could communicate to the reader the gravity of my previous two and a half years of the journey. As I reflected on everything I had written, I scrolled to the beginning of the book to read how the titles would be presented and their particular order. I had no intentions to change them, only to reflect on the way the story was told. And, if I ever was concerned that I had missed His message or misunderstood anything I had written, I would find one more great sign before me. The chapter of Genesis began on page 7. The chapter of Defining Moments – the last chapter that I had written over those days and wherein I defined Lindsey as the North Star, would begin on page 77. For if anything has become obvious to this point, it is that the number seven is God's method of communication and this was His spiritual confirmation that I had indeed heard His message correctly. For readers of this book, those chapters will ultimately begin on different page numbers because of formatting and page sizes, but in the draft

Best of Me

form, God let me know everything was right where it should be.

On the evening of the fifth day I was in Haiti – and the ending of the third day of my writing – I had an experience in the heavens that continued to offer me reassurance on the path with Lindsey. Though I was no longer questioning it in prayer, I suppose my soul must have needed hope and reassurance for the journey. It had been a week since she and I had last talked. Our last communication was when I let her know I would be gone for the next seven days to Haiti, to which I didn't receive a response. Not that it required one by any means, but I left for Haiti with a slight feeling of unresolve in our communication. But that evening I would experience a vision with a female angel that appears to me frequently when I am in the heavens. Though all of the supporting details are unimportant to recount here, both the female angel and a male angel escorted me around the heavens and talked to me about my spiritual growth. Near the end of the experience, they played a song for me – one I have never heard. The song played over and over again. The lyrics to the chorus rang out the strongest in my memory:

...

"Sundown nearing its end
And it's a fine time to see
That blue jean baby has got the best of me."

...

Gravity Calling

It was a song sung by three different male voices, each one singing a verse and a chorus in turn. Each voice was distinctly different, which I thought represented three different male archetypes (the Father, the Son, the Holy Ghost). It was a great song with a very catchy melody. But the importance was in what occurred while the song played. With each ringing out of the chorus, the angels continued to show me an image of Lindsey in blue jeans. Every time the chorus played, the female angel would electrify me with a jolt to let me know it was important. With each jolt, the image of Lindsey again appeared in the mind's eye of my soul. The jolt also triggered an intense feeling of passion inside, packaged in the overwhelming feeling of spiritual warmth. The overarching theme of the lyrics to the song was one of resolve in finding the "blue jean baby." The overall intention of this portion of my spiritual encounter was to grant my soul continued peace along the journey; a voice of reassurance after completing those all-too-important chapters of reflection from my journey thus far.

I began the following day by listening to music by Jim Brickman. His songs tend to send my soul on a ride wherein I can just observe the view. Inspired by the vision, I walked over to the restaurant ready to get my final day of writing underway. My fourth day of writing would be focused on fine tuning some of the final chapters to the book and making sure the themes flowed well throughout. While I ate breakfast, I removed my headphones. I checked multiple times to make sure I had paused the music, since I didn't want to drain the battery. Each time I verified my music was paused. So after I finished my breakfast, I pulled my headphones back out and was surprised to hear music playing. I must have laughed out loud at the moment because I already knew what was about to happen. I was going to look at the song name playing and it would be another seven and seven moment from God. I pulled my phone out of my pocket to see the song name. It was entitled "Wedding Bells." I couldn't help but smile. I also didn't know I had a song called "Wedding Bells" anywhere on my playlist, which made me laugh even more. Perhaps it was God just giving me a playful nudge in jest before my day of writing began. But, whatever the purpose in the action, I heard His voice and it made me smile. So that is how my day began.

My final day of writing ended with me writing the chapter "Before Good To See You Again." It was a necessary chapter of glue to Gravity Calling – and one that had found an unfinished holding place in the days prior. The portion of that chapter I focused on the most was on the section about anxiety and how it parallels to a child's emotions on Christmas Eve. As the day drew to a close, and after finalizing that important chapter, I walked over to where Rolf (the hotel owner) was sitting outside and made sure I could true up my balance for the food I had eaten throughout the day before leaving early in the morning. We walked over to another area on the property so I could pay. While we walked, Rolf talked about an incident that had occurred on one of his other properties in Haiti. He was eager to go see whatever the situation was. It was at this point he looked at me and said, "You know Jonathan, I feel like I am a child at Christmas. I can't wait to see my property.

Gravity Calling

I'm anxious." I stood there speechless, mesmerized at once again hearing God's voice – this time through Rolf. I laughed and joked about having just finished a chapter where I discussed that very point and I mentioned a few of the talking points. We had a good chuckle, I closed out my remaining balance and headed to bed not only inspired from the week of clarity, but also the recognition of God's voice in everything around me. It was occurring faster than it ever had. Or, perhaps I was just able to hear it better than I ever had before.

Only The Stars

On the seventh day of my journey, I awoke in the darkness of the night, again having had another series of spiritual experiences in the heavens. I had to wake up in the wee hours of the morning to make sure I made the cobbled journey around the countryside to reach my departing flight in time. I found myself waiting outside of the hotel facing the ocean with only the stars above. Even the hotel was blanketed in darkness for its generator went out throughout the night. There were no lights around to pollute the sky. It was the most brilliant view of the stars I had ever seen. I stood there for an hour soaking it all in as I waited for any mode of transportation to pass by. I prayed aloud thanking God for everything He had shown me on the trip and the mercy He had demonstrated to me in times when I lost my way. It was an extremely spiritual moment. In the poorest, most remote place I could be standing, I found myself looking at the beginning and end of creation in the sky, while having a conversation with God.

The return ride was filled with me silently observing the beautiful mess of Haiti. Everything was perfectly out of place, perfectly broken. On the long bus ride through the mountains, I found myself for the first time experiencing a spiritual and physical duality. There was a moment I had to question if the experiences from the heavens were in fact one-in-the-same as my earthly walk. One of the angels in particular that continues to recur throughout my experiences in the heavens appeared on the bus and smiled at me. And just as instantly, the angel was gone. I found myself debating which reality was the truth. Though I saw both experiences as separate truths, they were now blending into one. This was the start of a day that everything spoke to me. Every word. Every soul. I could see the souls of the Haitians around me that shined brighter than the rest – all speaking to me in song.

I arrived at the airport early, and found a bench to rest upon as I waited for my flight. As I waited, the seats in front of me filled up with a group of Americans all wearing blue shirts. They were obviously part of a mission trip of sorts. With my headphones on, I became aware that the group was talking about me – and not just about me. They were questioning who I was. One of the group leaders stared at me long enough to cause me to take my headphones off and see if they needed something from me. She just stared in disbelief at me. She said, "I'm sure you can tell we are talking about you. Are you him?"

I paused. This conversation was not of earthly origin. The words may be, but the thoughts driving the words were spiritual. This was the type of experience I have in the heavens. I just listened. She asked again, "Are you him? Are you the guy who arrived here alone and journeyed around by himself?" I acknowledged that I was. She then went on to tell me that we ran into each other my first day in Haiti. They were the only

Only The Stars

Americans I saw on that first day – the ones that were in disbelief I was backpacking alone. But her next words were even more important in the voice of the spirit. She said, "We didn't think you would make it. We didn't think you'd make it out alive. It is so great to see you."

The words were spoken like words from an angel in the heavens. I heard everything being told to me in both contexts – the spiritual parallel of self-discovery and the literal earthly meaning. I smiled and shared with them stories of my trip, the journey I had embarked on. We shared laughs and bonded. They found strength in my story, and I made sure to speak with a careful spiritual and earthly duality in all of the words that left my lips. As more members joined their group, they continued to talk about me and ask questions, even taking pictures to share my story with their friends. If this were an experience in the heavens, it would have been seen as a spiritual ceremony in recognition of understanding the journey and the purpose of this trip around the sun.

Eventually I was able to put my headphones back on and allow my mind to wonder again. I recalled the events of my flight down to Haiti and a particular lady I met on the flight. When we met, I could tell we had a spiritual recognition in each other. She let me borrow a pen when I filled out my paperwork for entering Haiti. But it was a particular part of our introductory conversation that continued to resonate in my head. Before we even formally introduced ourselves to each other, she told me somewhat randomly, "Someone is watching over you. It takes someone very special to do what you are doing." When she originally said the words, I recognized the spiritual overtones and the offbeat timing to the context of the situation, but now her voice rang out more clearly and with greater strength. In her words was the voice of God, letting me know I was taking the right steps on the journey.

In one last grand gesture from God before I left Haiti, I walked upstairs to get a quick bite to eat before the plane left. This time I was actually able to pay in cash and not use Haitian currency. All I wanted was a cheeseburger and fries – uncharacteristic of my usual cravings. I found a place in the food-court and ordered. The cashier rang me up – the total, $7.70. I couldn't help but smile. I paid and made sure to get a copy of the receipt. I returned back downstairs and boarded the plane.

On the first flight from Haiti to Miami, I chose to ride in silence. I wanted to focus only on my thoughts and meditate upon the events of the week. I had a layover in Miami for several hours, and I took that time to reread some of what I wrote while in Haiti. I decided not to turn on my cell phone or wifi until I stepped foot back in Nashville. That would be the official end to my sabbatical. Eventually it became time to board the plane and I decided to listen to the soundtrack to Man of Steel. I began listening to the twenty-minute piece called "Hans's Sketch" which included a mashup of all of the themes in the soundtrack. As we sat on the tarmac, I observed as all of the motions of the plane fell into synchrony with the song I was listening to. The moment the jets fired up was at the exact moment of a great crescendo in a song. The taxiing down the runway and the synchrony to a nature sequence playing on the drop down screens in the airplane all aligned precisely. I became so acutely aware of it, that I even scrubbed through parts of the track to disrupt timing. But nothing could have been any more divine than when the part of the theme, where in the movie Superman is shown with his fist raised in the air summoning all of his strength to fly through and destroy the world-drive machine that is slowly destroying Earth's atmosphere, was met in exact synchrony with an event in the physical world. At the precise microsecond in the song where Superman makes impact and destroys the machine, the man sitting in front of me launched his fist up into the air in synchrony and immediately pulled it down. I had to smile – nothing could have foreshadowed that moment. Nothing. Just as soon as the sound decayed from the climax and the next track began, the engines to the plane fired up in synchrony and we began our taxi down the runway. To some, the moments would have just happened to align in a happenchance sort of way. But to me, and with everything I had witnessed in the past seven days, it was divine synchrony played to the symphony of my soul.

    I arrived home and replied to my text messages. I checked three voicemails that all were from past friends reaching out to me with job opportunities. The last time I had a job opportunity fall into my lap was when I received the consulting opportunity I was currently in – this time there were three – a number that God would want me to recognize. I understood another change was coming in my career. Perhaps the job I

Gravity Calling

was in had run its course. Perhaps the job offer that was in the process of being finalized for my transition from consultant to full-time with my current employer would not happen, even though it had been announced to all of the staff multiple times in the preceding month. I wasn't sure what was to come, but change seemed obvious. Whatever the case may be, I found peace. After all, I had spent seven months consulting with my present employer – the timing definitely was in alignment.

I arrived home, showered, and crawled into bed. I wasn't tired, but the softness of my bed was inviting. I lay there reflecting on everything that had happened. I reread the notes I had taken from my travels to the heavens while I was in Haiti. Aside from the one that included Lindsey, they all seemed to focus on children or death. It was an odd series of experiences, but I knew they were all important, however disconcerting they were at the time. As I reread the journal entries, I realized they told a story. In each of the experiences I was an observer to something important I was intended to witness. It was only after seeing all of the experiences written about in succession that I realized they told a story that paralleled my personal and spiritual journey.

The final experience in the heavens that occurred on the seventh morning in Haiti bookended the first heavenly experience I had during the trip of meeting a young child who "wanted to be beautiful." On the fourth morning, I witnessed as a child and a random adult were killed. On the seventh morning – three days after the child and adult had died – I witnessed a funeral for someone of great importance in the

Only The Stars

heavens. There were two coffins – one was white and was paraded in celebration of the child who had died. The other was a black coffin where no one offered any remorse. It was larger, and housed an adult. Though no mention was made of the names or figures inside the coffins, I realized upon reflection that I was an observer to a story told about my very own spiritual journey. Over the seven days I watched as a child had to die – and did so with great celebration, while an adult also died with no remorse. The child represented my spirit, and its death represented its transition into a young adult no longer in divide. The adult who died represented my ego found housed within my earthly body. It was a ceremony of the greatest kind. The visions that I experienced in between, during the seven days, all foretold of a great celebration – a great event upcoming, one that would "divide the family." And by division, it indicated unity, pulling the ego out of its realm and putting it to rest. Throughout the week, I was continually told in the heavens that a child had to die and I couldn't quite rationalize the meaning. But in hindsight, the child was the youth of my spirit as my soul came into a greater understanding of All That Is and grew into a young adult.

It was in those moments of reflection I began to weep. I prayed. I thanked God for everything I was able to experience. Every seemingly insurmountable amount of joy and understanding that was revealed to me in Haiti and on my return home continued to be trumped by the next level of understanding revealed to me. Five years in desolation and nearly three years racing through the darkness toward light finally

Gravity Calling

had a blinding moment of clarity. I didn't think there could be any more divine encounters after that particular moment of understanding during the evening of the seventh day before I fell asleep – but God chose to communicate with me one more time. It was the grandest moment of my life.

Forevermore

The grandest moment of all of my life came in a response to an unspoken question in my final prayer of the evening. At this point, I'm sure my words have fallen short of how significant the experience of my call to visit Haiti was – though I've tried to paint the best picture I can with words as my palette of hues. The significance of the spiritual conversation I was having with God exceedingly blew my mind with every word He spoke...or perhaps it was in every word I heard, for I have to believe He has been speaking in this manner all of this time. But before my final prayer, I tried to allow my mind to find calm in the wake of understanding the child's death.

I began to tell God that for every word I said in prayer, I felt that it fell short in indicating my ability to hear His voice around me – and for that I asked for His patience with me. I asked that He help me be able to discern the change undoubtedly coming in my career. I told Him that I wanted to make sure I was following His path and not the path of money or entertaining the noise of the man with rose-colored glasses. I talked to Him about faith and how I realized the last part of the journey was intended for me to learn how to extinguish Anxiety from my thoughts. I acknowledged my faith in His plans for me, but I began to ramble on about how I hoped I would take the right actions in acknowledgement of His plans – and to take the right pacing for the journey to the Promised Land.

I must have rambled on for several minutes while I simultaneously prayed and thought aloud. I rambled about how in Deuteronomy, Moses and his tribes waited for God's instructions. I pondered if my action was to sit back and wait for further guidance in my career as well as with Lindsey. I also addressed needing help in discernment of waiting for His voice versus lack-of-initiative. I began thinking about how when my soul traverses the heavens, I seemed to have a universal understanding that God and the angels are ever-present and will appear when I call out for them. And even if I don't quite understand what I am doing in the heavenly experience all of the time, I am comforted and helped in times of need. And when I cannot understand a particular situation in the heavens and mess up in a test, everything is revealed as a step forward. There is never a punishment while reaching the destination – only learning, and it is all forever timeless.

But then I began to parallel the spiritual journey to the earthly walk and how one misstep – even if taken with a pure heart – can cause an avalanche of unforeseeable destruction. It was random babble and stream-of-consciousness, but eventually I was able to form the statement that I had a hard time understanding how to remove anxiety completely from my earthly walk in the same way I demonstrate faith in the heavens. I began to ask for guidance in helping me keep anxiety at bay and how to take the appropriate steps with Lindsey. I acknowledged I saw how He had aligned our paths to cross in this earthly walk and that I did not want to make a misstep. I wanted it to be as He planned it to be. As those last words came out of mouth, God helped me find resolve. I continued praying in a stream-of-consciousness fashion as the thought formed.

During the last several weeks of my journey, I had begun to understand the blending of the heavenly and earthly experiences into one. I started to get excited and see both experiences without division. I suddenly realized faith was to see and treat the earthly experience just as I treat my travels to the heavens. Every way I approach life on Earth must be done in the exact same manner. I don't fear in the heavens because I know I wield the protection of God. Though the man with rose-colored glasses leaves feelings of filth with the experiences, I know he can never hurt me. It doesn't make the experience any more or less desirable, but I know he cannot physically touch me. He can not lay a finger upon my soul, but only serve to introduce doubt and anxiety. As I came to this realization, the veil of both worlds was removed. I saw each for what they were as one. The lingering question about how to remove anxiety suddenly had resolve. As the words left my lips saying, "Perhaps faith is experiencing the earthly experiences just as I experience the heavenly experiences – to no longer see a divide but to see them as different perspectives of the same experience" my phone lit up with a text message.

I was so excited in recognition of the truth that God helped me see, but paused mid-sentence in reaction to my phone. I told God that I apologized, but I needed to check the phone to see if He was speaking to me. I glanced at my phone to find a message was from one of the past friends who had reached out to me wanting to setup a meeting for a job opportunity. I stopped and thought about who it was from before reading the message. I wondered if it was God acknowledging that this was the next step for my career. But, my question was founded on the details of its origination instead of stopping to see it for what it was. Then I read the message. All it said was: " :) "

My mind immediately jumped back to the random smiley face I had received from Bryan following his message about the bitter and sweet a couple of weeks prior. It was the mark of God's words between Bryan and me that day, so it was plausible that this message was more than just an acknowledgement to a specific job opportunity. My mind raced...and then I got it. I understood. I saw everything – the big picture, the small picture, and everything in between. It didn't matter who the text originated from. Perhaps it may hold significance to the job opportunity – that still remains to be seen. But in the spirit of how everything had been communicated to me over the past seven days, it was only – and solely – His voice. It was a response to my words. To put it into context, I said, "Perhaps faith is experiencing the earthly experiences just as I experience the heavenly experiences – to no longer see a divide but to see them as different perspectives of the same experience." And God replied with a smile.

Forevermore

At this point my face erupted in smile. I laughed. I was overcome with joy. Tears of happiness streamed down my face. God had replied directly in conversation to me in a fashion He knew I would understand. It was the moment that everything fell into view. It wasn't just about understanding the five acts of my journey. This was one step even greater. This was more than just the journey. It was a new spiritual destination. Through God, all things are possible – and in this moment I understood how. I understood faith. I only thought I understood faith leading up to that moment, and then the veil was removed. Every experience in the heavens and on Earth were necessary learning experiences for me on my journey so I could one day see how they apply simultaneously – for they are one. In that moment, the Spirit of The Lord filled my body and filled my soul with His warmth. I wept.

I wept uncontrollably for several minutes before being overcome in such a way that I could only roll out of bed and crawl onto the floor and find myself in complete worship of Him. My hands were outstretched above my head, my legs and chest pressed to the floor. Never had I been so overcome with anything in my life that I was taken to my knees in such a way that I was experiencing in that moment. In fact, I'm not sure I had ever before felt a desire to pray in that fashion outside of one or two symbolic times. But in this moment, I could not even remain in my bed in reverence, for it was too high above the floor to even breathe. I was drowning in an overflow of spiritual Love where I had to find myself face down, pressing my body against the floor in reverence to all that He Is just to find breath. I was naked, both literally and spiritually before Him, humbled in the moment; humbled in what He had revealed to me; humbled that I was shown His mercy to embark on the journey. There were no words that could be formed. Only tears of joy, of happiness, and reverence in Him. In every question, I now had answer, I had resolve. This was the shining moment where the sun rose above the horizon and began to shine down upon me – His light upon my flesh and upon my soul. It was a moment that I experienced for about an hour with uncontrollable tears and smiles, and one that I will continue to experience timelessly forevermore. For this was the great understanding that would give rise to my faith as I journeyed into the Promised Land. This was the end of the seventh day.

From The Sun

How does a person manage to walk in the earthly experience with the same eyes, heart, and soul as how the heavens are experienced? Without the experience of both to draw from, it may be hard for someone to fully understand what is about to be said. But, it all begins with this book. For within the words written, my soul is encased. The words have been written in every shade of midnight-red upon a canvas of the whitest of light. Every word, every pause, every breath in thought as the words are read, is the heartbeat of my soul. There will be a few blunders in my words, a few times my feet will get tangled up in racing toward the destination – but that is my soul; everything I am. Within the words is a rhythm – the pulse of divine inspiration racing through my veins like a rushing tide on a round-trip journey to and from the sun.

From the moments leading up to my Genesis and all of the way through to my Deuteronomy, each portion of this book was written at the same time period it was experienced, through the very lens of perspective experienced at that point in time. The heartache, the pain, the mix of emotions, the first rekindling of fire within, the first trip to the heavens to the most recent conversation with God – every word penned has placed my soul naked before every eye in the world to see, naked before the angels, and naked before God. It is a rebirth of a soul, painted in every hue of words, punctuation, pause, and word-play possible so that every soul who reads these words may find some version of recognition within – no matter what part of the journey they are on.

The beginning of the book will undoubtedly have seemed a little broken, perhaps a little disjointed, and influenced by a sense of pride holding on to those final moments preceding Genesis. Even after re-reading the book during proofing, that aspect stood out the greatest to me. But within the broken beginning, is the very mindset experienced while searching for any sense of understanding amidst the ruins of a marriage that had just fallen apart. The sense of wandering out of my encumbered darkness begins to appear within the experience of Genesis to Exodus, before I heard His voice, and through to the $77 found on my doorstep. By the eventual trip to Haiti, the clarity in the spiritual journey is echoed back in the clarity of the words – in recognition of standing in the desert no longer holding anyone's hand. The way it was written is the way it was intended through Him, for not only are the words important, but the mindset of the journey as well.

It is followed by an unbridled faith in God's plan – everything that He has foretold in the destination. Love was the first and the last. It was the beginning and the end of a journey unfolding in a way I never saw coming. No words could ever begin to sum up the way His all-consuming abundance of Love left me humbled on the floor, weeping in joy for an hour and no one around to see. Heading home from my trip to Haiti, my soul was left standing with feet buried in the sand, understanding everything the journey had been about, and laying witness to the Promised Land ahead. It was a point in time that marked my fifth act – my Deuteronomy – and where Anxiety took its last stand. The only thing remaining was to figure out how to run as fast as I could to the destination so that upon the day of my arrival, my soul and hers would feel the arc created in the same way He has demonstrated to me.

The one remaining stop on this portion of my journey is the concept of Love – and perhaps that is because the most important should be saved for last. We are all on a crash course with destiny. And while I may have once been a little reckless at times, the blazing trail I left behind illuminated a path of clarity of what once was and how I could learn to fly a little straighter, brave the headwind a little better, and find the space between two extreme pockets of air, passing through the eye of His needle where the ride is smooth and tranquil – where only in the periphery is the chaos of the world around us recognizable. For everything in our earthly walk has a rhyme and a reason, building character, and helping growth for each and every soul. And though at times early in the journey it may seem to conflict with what we have envisioned in our minds, we must all learn that our ego-driven thoughts do not hold a glimmer to the plans God has envisioned for us. We are all eternal, bound by a finite earthly body, experiencing the journey in the tiniest speck of time in the great expanse of All That Is. Our soul's voice is there to reassure us in how everything great falls outside of the bounds of time and our earthly walk.

    In the recent weeks, I had just begun to get to know the girl that had illuminated the heavens with the brightest of lights when her soul and mine collided over three and a half years ago. I would begin to notice during each Sunday church service we attended together that certain words the pastor would say and certain themes he would discuss, would cause her eyes to well up with tears in recognition of the message touching her soul in the wake of her own personal journey. Her hurt left her soul delicate. The casual touches at the corners of her eyes to prevent her makeup from running or letting me know that her emotions were spilling out in recognition of the pastor's words, gave her away. Themes of forgiveness and moving on were the ones that touched her the most.

    It was evident that in every shade of beautiful she radiated sitting next to me, and as beautiful as her stained glass pattern was that bathed the church walls everyday we sat together, our proximity was not the indication of reaching the destination. It was still just a step along the journey. Sitting next to each other in the house of God with souls in song may be the single closest place two physical bodies can be in witness before God. But as close in proximity as we were, each day I would come home and pray for God to let her soul know that I was running as fast as I could to her and to have faith that I knew she was running as fast as she could to me, in the way that only she could do. It was the space between our souls running toward each other that would prove to be the story yet untold

From The Sun

about the journey from that place in the sand I found myself standing and the Promised Land that remained ahead.

There was a song my soul felt every time she was near. And I know her soul heard it as well. But there were still a few remaining steps to take on my journey before my soul could be best prepared for all that was foretold. On that seventh day when I returned home from Haiti, I would come to learn that those steps would involve leaving my body behind in action, feet in the sand, staring at the Promised Land. For that is as close as an earthly body can ever be in the experience of Love. It is only a view from afar. And as close as Lindsey and I sat each day together in church, that would only be as close figuratively as we would ever become before my soul could cross the desert into the Promised Land, in the way my King intended for me – as well as for her. So, with bare feet pressed into the sand, Promised Land in sight, the rising sun pouring every ounce of its abundant light onto my flesh and my soul, it became a lesson in understanding not just how to have unbridled faith, but to demonstrate it in a fashion that radiates every bit of light back into the world that He shined down upon my soul when she fell into view. It would begin with this book – by encasing my soul in words so that those of earthly mind could see my soul in the same light as I see them, and in the same light as I experience the heavens – completely pure, soul complexly naked, an overflowing abundance of all I have to give, seen through eyes like a child – full of wonder, full of light; with a heart full of passion – a fire-alive, raging unconditionally, ferociously inside. It would end with me standing with my

Gravity Calling

earthly feet buried in the physical sand here on Earth, but one last great chapter remained.

Spellstruck

And so as this portion of my journey draws to an end, the final chapter begins with Lindsey reading this book for the first time. No other eyes will have seen it before hers. At a coffee shop, Lindsey will have received the copy of the book professionally bound and printed specifically for her. Our meeting at the coffee shop will have not seemed to have any intention other than random conversation – catching up about our pasts, so the book will be somewhat unexpected to see. It will come with no explanation, no foreshadowing of what she will read. It will likely have been our first meeting outside of our church visits, so it would seem likely that the conversation could entail how we first met. If that is the case, I will no doubt tell her the reason I remembered our first encounter with words that allude to the way it is described in this book, but with fewer details so as not to spoil the chapters. It will undoubtedly be something along the lines of "...because while I was trying to paint the world in happiness in the midst of my pain, you managed to paint mine. Your smile became my favorite smile. It left me inspired and I wrote about it." Those are words I've waited to say to her for three and a half years, but we will see if that actually gets to be the case.

Gravity Calling

At this point, she will have just read those words and be reflecting back on whether that topic of conversation came up. Maybe it did. Maybe it didn't. But I would like to believe she is smiling either way right now. Regardless, that is what I want to believe is happening at this very moment because I have remembered her smile every day since we met, and I'd like to think her smile is lighting up her face right now as she reads these words. It will always be my favorite smile. She will probably now be thinking about how our meeting was much more architected in design than it seemed – and if she wasn't, she now definitely is after reading these words. She will think about two additional items she received along with the book that day. The first was a bookmark that was placed inside of the book as it was handed to her. Hopefully, the bookmark is still in the book, because there is something very special about it. Aside from the bookmark having one of her favorite Bible verses printed on it, when she turns it over she will notice there is fabric sewn onto the back of the leather. It looks like the bookmark was made with it, but it wasn't. The fabric was stitched in place to conceal something very important inside. In other words, it is meant to be removed – but it will likely take a little bit of work to remove it – my tailor did a great job making it look factory made. So now, she has probably flipped the bookmark over and is picking at it, seeing if she can pull it apart without having to get up and go get a knife or scissors. Spoiler alert: she will have to get up and get scissors.

When she manages to pull the fabric away, she will find a folded up piece of paper. On that piece of paper is a poem that

Spellstruck

came to me as I was about to jump in the shower before a New Year's party I was getting ready to attend – all before I ever said "good to see you again." The moment she and I first met was rambling through my mind as I turned the shower water on and began to step my first foot into the shower. But like a bolt of lighting hitting me in the same way it occurred the day Lindsey and I first met, my mind was filled in words and verse in a completed form so quickly, that I immediately had to turn the shower off and write it down.

The words that she will read are the first words I would write about her after having written about her the day we first met three and a half years ago. Each pen-stroke as I wrote the words to the poem felt like it was permanently being chiseled into the aether around me – or perhaps it already had been at some point before and I was just tracing the groove marks left behind. Certainly at this point she will be reading the poem and the words will be sinking in.

After she returns back from the poem to continue reading this chapter, with absolute certainty, she is now thinking about the last item she received that day at the coffee shop. This item was a coffee mug. While it would not be particularly evident in any way, I had this mug handmade for her. Depending on how the events actually played out at the coffee shop that day, the plan was for me to arrive early and have her favorite cup of coffee waiting for her before she arrived. But instead of the typical paper cups most coffee shops use, hers would be waiting for her in this mug. I would make a joke about having seen it earlier in the day and decided to pick it up for her having thought it would be something she would like. I would have given some excuse about how no one likes to drink coffee out of a paper cup anyway. We would have laughed and that would be the way she came into possession of the coffee mug. Perhaps she is even drinking coffee out of it right now while she is reading these words. If so, it is going to make for a messy situation because she is going to have to break the mug at this point in the story. This mug is going to need to be shattered into a million pieces because within the clay that was used to make the mug, a key was carefully placed inside so as not to be noticed. My best guess is the key is located in the base, but she's going to have to figure that part out on her own. The key is to a safety deposit box located at SunTrust Bank in Green Hills, Tennessee – right down the road from her place of work. The contents inside are for her specifically. As she reads these final words, she will find one last message in closing from me, addressed directly from my soul to hers.

Lindsey,

At this point, I hope you are not the type of person to read the ending of a story first, because if you did, you will have discovered that the last several chapters beyond this page are from The Great Gatsby...*which I'm sure would have been a little confusing. But I couldn't take the risk of you reading this chapter before any of the others. It needed to arrive in the order it did, so that you would find yourself having just finished reading these words, sitting amidst the remnants of a bookmark that once was and the shattered pieces of a coffee mug, with a key in your hand. And though I*

Spellstruck

know there is a lot to be taken in from all I have written – enough to leave a person spellstruck for a while as it all lingers in the mind – find calm in knowing that it is a song timeless in design. If anything should be apparent at this point, it is that there is a delicacy and grace in all that I have done, and that will remain the case in all that I will ever do. When you arrive at the bank with the key, ask for Sara Dudley. She will see to it that you are taken care of the rest of the way from here.

Always,
Jonathan

...

Peace be with you and may you find within these words a truth that finds resonance within your soul.

...

www.ingramcontent.com/pod-product-compliance
Lightning Source LLC
Chambersburg PA
CBHW021139080526
44588CB00008B/132